THE POCK

THE POCKET EASY SPELLER

CLAREMONT BOOKS

PENGUIN BOOKS

Published by the Penguin Group
Penguin Books Ltd, 27 Wrights Lane, London W8 5TZ, England
Penguin Books USA Inc., 375 Hudson Street, New York, New York 10014, USA
Penguin Books Australia Ltd, Ringwood, Victoria, Australia
Penguin Books Canada Ltd, 10 Alcorn Avenue, Toronto, Ontario, Canada M4V 3B2
Penguin Books (NZ) Ltd, 182–190 Wairau Road, Auckland 10, New Zealand

Penguin Books Ltd, Registered Offices: Harmondsworth, Middlesex, England

First published by Whitcoulls Publishers, Auckland, NZ 1987
Published in Penguin Books 1994

This edition published by Claremont Books,
an imprint of Godfrey Cave Associates Limited,
42 Bloomsbury Street, London WC1B 3QJ,
under licence from Penguin Books Ltd, 1995

ISBN 1 85471 769 3

INTRODUCTION

Have you ever needed to know the correct spelling of a particular word, but either didn't have a dictionary with you or couldn't be bothered wading through all the information in a standard dictionary? *The Pocket Easy Speller* can solve your spelling problems. Here is an alphabetical listing of the most commonly misspelt words in everyday use – a pocket-sized, easy-to-use spelling reference for home, school and the office.

How to Use *The Pocket Easy Speller*
■ *The Pocket Easy Speller* lists close to 12,000 words in alphabetical order.
■ Italics have been used to help you remember spellings. Often a related word is 'buried' in a word; for example, in access*ible* is the word access, in account-*able*, the word account. These buried words have been highlighted by italicizing what is left. When you are spelling the word access*ible*, thinking of access may help you with the longer word.
■ Square brackets have been used to indicate plurals that are *not* formed by the addition of 's' to the singular noun, for example, vertex [tices].
■ Where word forms might be confused, the following abbreviations have been included: **n** (noun), **v** (verb),

a (adjective), **prep.** (preposition), **s** (singular), **p** (plural), **f** (feminine), **m** (masculine). For example, a word may change its form slightly when it becomes another part of speech (pastoral **a**, pastorale **n**) or when it changes gender (fiancé **m**, fiancée **f**); it may function as more than one part of speech (rout **n/v**); or it may be a singular or plural spelling, or both (chassis **s/p**).

- Wordbreaks, indicated by a diagonal stroke, have been inserted to assist with deciding how to split a word over two lines. Only major breaks have been given; other breaks are possible. In breaking words, care should be taken to preserve the pronunciation and visual recognition of the whole word. In general it is recommended that at least two letters should be left at the end of a line and at least three letters taken over to the next line, for example super/fici/ality.

- Italics have also been used to indicate those words of foreign origin that have not, as yet, been completely assimilated into current English. In this case you will find the whole word is in italics, for example, *fait accompli*.

- The use of ↔ indicates homonyms – words having the same spellings or sounds but different meanings.

A

aba/cus
aba/lone
aban/doned
abase/ment
abashed
abate/ment
ab/at/toir
ab/besses
abbeys
abbot
ab/brevi/ated
ab/brevi/ation
abdic/ated
ab/domen
abdom/inal
ab/duction
ab/errant
ab/erra/tion
abetted
abet/ter
abet/tor
abey/ance
abhor/rence
abide
abil/ity
ab/jectly
ab/jured
ablu/tions
ably
abneg/ation
ab/normal/ity
abode
abolish/able
aboli/tion

abomin/able
aborigin/ality
Abori/gines
abort/ively
abra/cadabra
abraded
abras/ive
abreast
abridge
abridge/ment
abroad
abrog/ated
abruptly
abs/cess
ab/sconder
ab/sence
absentee/ism
ab/sinth
abso/lutely
absolu/tion
ab/solved
absorb/able
absorb/ency
absorb/ent
ab/sorption
ab/stained
abstemi/ously
absten/tion
abstin/ence
ab/straction
ab/strusely
absurd/ity
abund/ance
abuse n/v
abus/ive/ness
abut/ment
abutted

abys/mally
abyss
acacia
academic/ally
aca/demi/cian
acceded
accel/era/tion
acceler/ator
accentu/ated
accept/able
accept/ance
ac/ceptor
access/ible
access/ories p
access/ory
acci/dence
accident/ally
ac/claimed
acclama/tion
acclimat/ized
accliv/ity
accol/ade
accom/moda/
     tion
accom/pani/
     ment
accompan/ist
accom/plice
accomplish/
     ment
accord/ance
accor/dion
ac/costed
account/able
account/ancy
account/ant
accoutre/ments

ac/credit/able
ac/credited
accre/tion
accrued
accumu/lation
accumu/lator
accur/acy
accur/ate
ac/cursed
ac/cusal
accusat/ively
accusat/ory
accused
accus/tomed
acet/ate
acetic
acet/one
acetyl/ene
ached
achiev/able
achieve/ment
achrom/atic
acid/ity
acid/osis
acidu/lated
acknowledge
acknowledge/
     ment
acme
acne
aco/lyte
acoustic/ally
acquaint/ances
acquies/cence
ac/quired
ac/quisi/
     tive/ness

acquit/*tal*	ad/equate*ly*	adsorp/tion	affer/ent
acquit/*tance*	adher/*ence*	adu/latory	affian/ce*d*
acre/*age*	adhes/ive	adulter/ate*d*	affi/davit
acrid	ad hoc	adul/tery	affili/ation
ac/ri/moni/*ously*	adieus	advance/ments	affin/ity
acri/mony	adipos/ity	advantage/*ously*	affirmat/ive*ly*
acro/batic/*ally*	ad/jacent	adventi/tious*ly*	af/flict*ion*
acro/polis	adject/ive	adverbi/al*ly*	afflu/ence
across	adject/iv/al*ly*	advers/ary	afford*ed*
acros/tic/*ally*	adjourn/*ment*	adversat/ively	afforesta/*tion*
ac/rylic	adjudic/ator	advers/ity	affrays
action/*able*	adjunct/*ive*	advert/ised	af/fright*ed*
act*iv*/*ity*	adjured	advertise/*ment*	af/front*ed*
act*or*	adjust/*ment*	advice **n**	Afghan
act/ress*es*	adminis/ter*ed*	advisab/ility	afraid
actu/al*ity*	adminis/trator	advised **v**	Afric/an/*ism*
actu/al*ly*	admir/able	advis/ory	Afri/kaans
actu/ary	admir/al*ty*	advoc/ate*d*	Afri/kaner
actu/ate*d*	admira/tion	adze	after/math
acu/ity	admiss/ible	aegis	agar
acumen	admit/*table*	aeon	agate
acumin/ate*d*	admit/*tance*	aer/ate*d*	age
acute*ly*	ad/mitted*ly*	aeri/al*ly*	age/ing
adage	admonish/*ment*	aerie *use* eyrie	agency
adamant/*ine*	admoni/tion	aero/batics	agenda
adapt/*abil*/*ity*	admonit/ory	aero/drome	agglom/era/tion
adap*ter*	ado	aero/dynamic*s*	agglu/tin/ate*d*
adden/dum [da]	adobe	aero/naut*ical*	aggrand/ize*d*
ad/dict*ion*	adoles/cence	aero/planes	ag/gra/vate*d*
addi/tion/al*ly*	adoles/cent	aes/thetic/*ally*	aggreg/ate*d*
addit/ive	adopt/*ive*	aeti/ology	ag/gressor
addle*d*	ador/ably	affa/bil/ity	ag/grieve*d*
ad/dress*ee*	adora/tion	affable	aghast
adduc/ible	adorn/*ment*	affair	agile*ly*
aden/oid*al*	adren/alin	affect	agil/ity
adept	adroit*ly*	affect*a/tion*	agit/ator
ad/equacy	adsorb*ed*	affection/ate*ly*	ag/nostic/*ism*

agog
agon/ize*d*
agora/phobia
ag/rarian
agree/*able*
agreed
agri/cultur/al*ly*
aid*ed*
aide-de-camp
ail/eron
Aire/dale
aisle
akimbo
alabas/ter
à la carte
alac/rity
alarm
alarum
Alba/nia*n*
alba/tross
al/beit
albi/nos
album
albu/men
albumin/ous
alchem/ist
al/chemy
alco/holics
alcove
alde/hyde
alder/man
alert/*ness*
al/fresco
algebra/*ically*
alias*es*
alibi*s*
alien/*able*

alien*ate*
align/*ment*
alike
aliment/ary
ali/mony
ali/quot
alkal/in*e*
all right
Allah
allay*ed*
allega/tion
alleg*ed*
allegi/ance
alleg/ory
alle/luia *also*
  halle/lujah
al/lergic
al/lergy
allevi/ate*d*
alley
alli/ance
alliga/tor
alliter/ation
alloc/ate*d*
allot/*ment*
allot/*tee*
allo/trope
allow/*able*
allow/*ance*
allow*ed*
al/lude*d*
al/lure*d*
allu/sion
allu/vial
allu/vium
ally [allies]
al/manac

al/mond
almost
alms
aloe*s*
aloof
aloud
alpaca
alpha/betic/al*ly*
al*pine*
al/ready
altar
alter/*able*
alter*ed*
altercation
alterna/tive*ly*
al/though
alti/meter
alti/tude
al/together
altru/ism
alu/minium
always
amal/gam/ator
amanu/ensis
  [ses]
amar/anth
amass*ed*
ama/teur/*ish*
amat/ory
amaze/*ment*
ambassad/or*ial*
amber/gris
ambi/dextrous
ambigu/ity
ambigu/ous*ly*
ambi/tious*ly*
ambro/sia*l*

ambu/lance
ambus/cade
ambush*ed*
amelior/ate*d*
amen/able
amend/*able*
amen/ities
Amer/ican/*ism*
amethyst
ami/abil/ity
ami/able
amic/ably
amity
am/meter
ammoni/ate*d*
ammuni/tion
am/nesia
am/nesty
amoeba*s*
amok *also*
  amuck
among
amoral
am/or/ous*ly*
amorph/ous*ly*
amort/ize*d*
amount*ed*
ampere
amphi/bian
amphi/theatre
ampli/fica/tion
ampli/tude
am/poule
ampu/tate*d*
amu/let
amuse/*ment*
anabol/ism

4

anachron/ism
ana/condas
an/aemia
an/aemic
anaer/obe
anaes/thesia
anaes/thetic
an/algesia
anal*ly*
ana/logous*ly*
ana/logue
ana/logy
ana/lys*ed*
ana/lysis [yses]
ana/lyst
analytic/al*ly*
an/archy
ana/themat/iz*ed*
anatomic/al*ly*
an/cestor
ances/try
anchor/*age*
anchor/ite
an/chovy
an/cient
ancil/lary
and/iron
andro/gyn/ous
anec/dote
anec/dotal
anemone
aner/oid
angel*ic*/al*ly*
an/gelus
angina
angl*ed*
Anglican/*ism*

Angli/ciz*ed*
Anglo-Saxon
angora
an/grily
angry
an/guish*ed*
angular/*ity*
anil/ine
animal/*ity*
anim/at*ed*
animos/ity
anion
ani/seed
ank/le*t*
annals
anneal*ed*
annexe **n** *also*
    annex
annex **v**
annihil/at*ed*
anni/vers/ary
Anno Domini
annot/at*ed*
announce/*ment*
annoy/*ance*
annu/al*ly*
annu/ity
annu/lar
an/nul*led*
annul/*ment*
annunci/ation
anode
ano/dyne
anoint*ed*
anomal/ous*ly*
anom/aly
anonym/ity

anonym/ous*ly*
answer/*able*
ant/agon/ist*ic*
Ant/arctic*a*
ante meridiem
ante/cedent
ante/dat*ed*
ante/dilu/vian
ante/lope
ante/nat/al*ly*
an/tenn*ae*
anthem
anther
antho/logy
anthra/cite
an/thrax
anthrop/oid
anthropo/logy
anthropomorph/
    ous
anti/biotic
antic
anti/cipat/ory
anti/climax
anti/cyclone
anti/dote
anti/gen
anti/logar/ithm
anti/mony
anti/nomy
anti/pathy
anti/podes
antiquar/ian
an/tiques
an/tiquity
antir/rhinum
anti-/Semitic

anti/septic
anti/strophe
anti/thesis
antiven/ene
antler*ed*
ant/onym
anvil
anxiety
anxious*ly*
Anzac
aorta
apache (A)
apart/heid
apart/*ment*
apathetic/al*ly*
aperi/ent
aper/itif
aper/ture
apex*es or* apices
apha/sia
aphis [aphides]
aphor/ism
aphro/disiac
apiary
apiece
apish
aplomb
apoca/lypse
apo/cryph*al*
apo/gee
apolo/getic
apolo/giz*ed*
apo/logy
apo/plectic
apo/plexy
apos/tasy
apostle

apo/stolic
apo/strophe
apothec/ary
apothe/osis
appal/lingly
appar/atuses
ap/parelled
appar/ently
appari/tion
ap/pealed
appeal/ing
appear/ance
appease/ment
appel/lant
append/age
appendi/citis
ap/pendixes *or*
   ap/pendices
apper/tained
appet/izer
appet/iz/ing
appet/ite
ap/plauded
ap/plause
appli/ance
applic/able
applic/ant
applied
appli/qué
appoint/ment
appor/tioned
ap/posi/tion/ally
ap/praisal
appre/ciable
appre/ciably
appreci/atively
appre/hended

appre/hens/ible
appren/ticed
apprentice/ship
ap/prised
approach/able
approba/tion
appropri/ately
ap/proval
approxim/ated
ap/proxim/ately
appurten/ance
apri/cot
apron
apro/pos
apti/tude
aqua/marine
aqua/plane
aquar/iums *or*
   aquar/ia
aquatic
aque/duct
aque/ous
aquil/ine
arab/esque
Ara/bian
arable
ar/biter
arbit/rary
arbit/rator
arbor/eal
arc
arcade
archae/ology
ar/chaic
arch/angel
arch/ery
arche/type

archi/pelagos
archi/tectural
archi/tecture
archi/trave
arch/ives
Arctic
ardent*ly*
ardour
ardu/ously
area
arenas
Argen/tine
argu/ably
argued
argu/ing
argu/ment*at/ive*
arias
arid/ity
aristo/cracy
arith/metical
ark
armadas
arma/dillos
Arma/geddon
arma/ture
armis/tice
ar/mourer
aro/matic
aroused
arque/buses *use*
   harque/buses
arraign/ment
arrange/ment
arrant
arrayed
arrears
ar/rested

ar/rival
arrog/antly
ar/senal
arsen/ical
arson/ist
arte/fact
arter/ial
artery
arte/sian
arth/ritis
arthro/pod
arti/choke
art/icled
articu/late
arti/fact *use*
   arte/fact
arti/ficially
artil/lery
ar/tisan
artistic/ally
arum
as/bestos
ascend/ant (*ent*)
ascen/sion
ascent
ascer/tain/able
ascetic/ally
ascribed
aseptic
ashen
Asi/atic
asin/ine
askance
askew
aspar/agus
aspect
asper/ity

asper/sion
as/phalt*ed*
asphyxi/*ated*
aspic
aspi/distra
aspir/ant
aspir/ate
aspira/tion
aspirin
assail/*able*
assail/*ant*
assassin/at*ed*
as/sault*ed*
assay/*able*
as/sembly
as/sent*ed*
as/sert*ed*
assess/*able*
assess/*ment*
as/sess*or*
asset*s*
assidu/ity
assign/*ment*
assimil/*able*
assimil/at*ed*
assist/*ance*
assist/*ant*
assize*s*
associ/ation
associat/ive
asson/ance
as/suag*ed*
as/sum*ed*
assump/tion
assur/ance
aster/*isk*
aster/*oid*

asth/ma*tic*
astigmat/ism
astonish/*ment*
as/tound/ing*ly*
astra/khan
astrin/gent
astro/loger
astro/nomic/al*ly*
astute/*ness*
asylum
asymmet/rical
asym/metry
atav/istic
athe/istic/al*ly*
ath/lete
ath/let/ic*ism*
athwart
atlas*es*
atmo/sphere
at/mo/spheri/
    cal*ly*
atoll
atom*ic*
atom/iz*er*
atone/*ment*
atro/cious*ly*
atro/city
atrophy/*ing*
at/taché
attach/*ment*
attain/*able*
at/tempt*ed*
attend/*ance*
atten/tion
attent/ive*ly*
attenu/at*ed*
attesta/*tion*

attic
atti/tude
attor/neys
attract/ive*ly*
attrib/utable
attri/tion
attuned
au pair
au revoir
auburn
auction/*eer*
auda/cious*ly*
aud/ibly
audi/ence
audit/orium
aud/itory
auger
aug/menta/*tion*
augur
aura
aur/al*ly*
aure/ole
aur/icle
aurifer/ous
au/roras
aus/pic*es*
auspi/cious*ly*
aus/tere*ly*
Aus/tra/lasia*n*
Aus/tra/lia*n*
authentic/al*ly*
authentic/*ate*
author/*ess*
author/iz*ed*
authoritat/ive
author/ity [ties]
auto/bio/graphy

auto/cracy
auto/cratic/*ally*
auto/graph*ed*
auto/matic
automa/tion
auto/matons or
    auto/mata
auto/mobile
auto/nomous*ly*
aut/opsy
au/tumna*l*
aux/ili/ary
avail/*able*
avail*ed*
ava/lanche
avant-garde
avari/cious*ly*
avatar
aveng*ed*
avenue*s*
aver/ag*ed*
aver/*ment*
averr*ed*
aver/sion
avert/*ible*
avi/ary
avi/ator
avid/*ly*
avoca/do*s*
avoca/tion
avoid/*able*
avoid/*ance*
avoirdu/pois
avowa*l*
avuncu/lar
aware/*ness*
aweigh

awe/struck
aw/fully
awk/ward/ness
awl
awn/ing
awry
axi/ality
axil/lary
axio/matic
axis [axes]
axle
axo/lotl
azaleas
azure

B

Baal
bab/bler
babel
baboon
Babylon/ian
Bacchan/alia
Bac/chic
bach/elor
bacil/lus [lli]
back/ward
bacon
bacterio/phage
bac/terium [ria]
bade
badgered
badin/age
bad/minton
baga/telle
bag/gage

bailed
bail/iff
baited
baize
bake/lite
bala/clava (B)
bala/laika
bal/ance/able
bal/cony
bale
balked ↔
    baulked
bal/lade
bal/ladry
bal/lasted
baller/inas
ballet
bal/listics
bal/locks also
    bol/locks
balloon/ist
bal/loted
balmy
balsa
balsam
balus/traded
bam/boos
banal/ity
bananas
band/aged
ban/dan(n)a
ban/deaux
ban/died
ban/ditti
bando/lier also
    bando/leer
bandy

bane/fully
banish/ment
ban/ister
banjoes or
    banjos
bank/ruptcy
banned
bannered
banns
ban/queted
ban/shee
bantam
Bantu
banyan
bao/bab
bap/tized
baptis/mal
baptist/ery also
    baptist/ry
barbar/ian
barbar/ity
barbar/ously
barbe/cued
barber
barbitur/ate
bar/carole also
    bar/carolle
bare/faced
barely
bar/gained
bargee
bari/tone
bar/ium
bark
barley
barn/acles
barney

baro/meter
baron/ess
bar/onet
baro/nial
baroque
barra/cudas
bar/rage
bar/relled
bar/ren/ness
barri/caded
bar/rier
bar/rister
barrow
bartered
basal
basaltic
base
base/ment
basic/ally
basil
basil/ica
basi/lisk
basis [bases]
bask
basket/ware
basque
bass
bas/sinet ↔ bas/
    sinette
bassoon/ist
bas/tardy
basted
bas/tille (B)
bas/tion
bated
bath n
bathe v

bathos
bathy/sphere
batik
baton
bat/talion
bat/ten*ed*
bat/tery
battle/dore
bauble
baulk*ed* ↔
  balk*ed*
baux/ite
bawdi/ness
bawdy
bayon/et*ed*
bayou
bazaar
ba/zooka
beach/comber
beach-/head
beacon
bead/*ing*
beadle
beagle
beaker
beanie
bear/*able*
beard*ed*
beast*li*/ness
beat
beati/fica/*tion*
beati/tude
beauteous
beauti/ful*ly*
beauti/fy*ing*
beauty
beckon*ed*

becom/ing/*ness*
bedevil/*ment*
bedlam/*ite*
bed/ouin (B)
  s/p
be/draggl*ed*
beech
Beel/zebub
beetle
beet/root
be/fit*ted*
before/hand
beget/*ting*
beg/gary
begin/*ning*
be/gonia
be/grudg*ed*
be/guil*ed*
be/guine
behavi/our/*ism*
beige
be/lated
belay*ed*
be/leaguer*ed*
belfry
Bel/gian
belief*s*
believ/able
be/lieve
bella/donna
belle
bel/letrist
bellicos/ity
belli/gerence
bel/low*ed*
belly/*ful*
bemus*ed*

be/neath
bene/dict/ory
bene/factor
bene/ficence
bene/ficial*ly*
bene/fit*ed*
bene/volence
benign
benig/nant*ly*
ben/ison
benumb*ed*
benze/drine (B)
ben/zene
ben/zine
be/queath*ed*
be/quest
bereave/*ment*
beret
ber/serk
berth*ed*
beryl/lium
be/seech/*ing*
be/sieg*ed*
be/sought
besti/al*ly*
beta/*tron*
bête noire
betel
be/tray*al*
be/troth*al*
bev/el*led*
bever/age
bevy [bevies]
beware
bewilder/*ment*
be/witch/*ing*
bey

bias*ed also*
  bias*sed*
Bible
bib/lical
biblio/graphy
biblio/phile *also*
  bibliophil
bibu/lous
bi/cameral
bi/carbon/ate
bi/centen/ary
bi/centen/nial
biceps
bi/chlor/ide
bi/chrom/ate
bicyc/list
bid/*dable*
bi/ennial
bier
bi/focal
bifurc/ated
bigam/ous
bight
bigot*ry*
bikinis
bi/later/al*ly*
bilge
bi/lingu/al*ly*
bilious/*ness*
bilk*ed*
billet-doux
billet*ed*
bil/liard*s*
bil/lowy
billy
binary
bin/aural

binge
bin/ocu/lars
bi/nomial
bio/chemistry
bio/graphical
bio/logical
bio/physics
bio/plasm
bi/par/tisan
bi/par/tite
bi/pedal
bi/polar
birch
bi/retta
birth/place
bis/cuit
bi/sector
bish/op/ric
bison
biting
bit/tern
bitu/men
bitumin/ized
bitumin/ous
bivou/acked
bi/zarre
black/guardly
black/mailer
blad/der
blame
blame/able
blame/less
blanched
blanc/mange
blandish/ment
blan/keted
blared

blasé
blas/phemed
blasphem/ously
blas/phemy
bla/tancy
bla/tantly
blazer
blaz/oned
blaz/onry
bleached
bleakly
blear/ily
bleat/ing
bleed/ing
blem/ished
blighted
bliss/fully
blithely
bliz/zard
bloated
bloc
block/ade
blond m
blonde f
blos/somed
blouse
blowzi/ness
blowzy
blub/bered
bludgeoned
blue/ing
blu/ish
blunder/busses
blurb
blurred
blurted
boar

boarder
boas
boast/fully
boat/swain
bob/bin
bobsleigh
bodice
bodi/less
bod/kin
Boer
bogeys also
   bogy [bogies]
bogie
bogus
bogy [bogies]
Bo/hemian
boister/ously
bolder
bole
bol/locks also
   bal/locks
Bol/shevik
bol/stered
bombard/ier
bom/bastic/ally
bona fides n
bon/anza
bond/age
bon/fire
bon/homie
boni/est
bon/neted
bonny
bonuses
bony
boom/erang
boor

bootees
booty
bor/acic
bordered
bore
born
borne
boron
borough
bosom
bo'sun
bot/an/ically
botu/lism
bou/doir
bough
bought
bouil/lon
boul/der
bou/levard
bouncing
bound/ary
boun/teously
bounti/fully
bou/quet
bourgeoisie
boutique
bowdler/ized
bowed
bowels
bowl
boy/cotted
brace/let
bra/chial
bracken
brack/eted
brack/ish
brag/gart

Brahmin/*ism*
braid*ed*
braille (B)
brainy
braised
brake
brandy
bras/sière
brav/ado*es*
bravo*s*
bra/vura
brazen
brazen/*ness*
bra/zier
Brazil/*ian*
breach*ed*
breadth
break/*able*
break/fast*ed*
bream
breast*ed*
breath **n**
breath/alyser
breath*ed*
breath/ing
breech*es*
breezi/ness
breezy
brethren
breve
brevi/ary
brev/ity
briar
bribe*ry*
bric-à-brac
bridal
bridle

brief*ly*
bri/gade
brigad/ier
brigand/*age*
brilliant/*ine*
brine
briny
bri/quette *also*
   briquet
bristly
Brit/ain
Britan/nia
Brit/ish
Briton
Brit/tany
brittle/*ness*
broach*ed*
broad/cast
bro/cad*ed*
broc/coli
bro/chure
brogue
broker/*age*
brom/ide
bron/chi*tis*
broncos
bronto/saurus
bronz*ed*
brooch*es*
brougham
brouhaha
brown/*ness*
browse*d*
bruise*d*
bruit*ed*
bru/nette
brusque*ly*

brutal/*ity*
buccan/eer*ed*
bucolic/*ally*
Bud/dhism
budger/igar
budget/*ary*
budget*ed*
buffa/lo*es*
buffet
buf/fet*ed*
buf/foon
bulb/*ous*
bulging
bul/letin
bul/lion
bul/lock
bul/rush*es*
bul/wark
bump/tious*ly*
bunga/low
bunion
Bunsen
buoy/*ant*
bur ↔ burr
burden*ed*
bureau/*cracy*
bur/ette
bur/geon*ed*
burglar
bur/gundy
burial
buried
bur/lesque*d*
burly
burn/ish*ed*
burr ↔ bur
bur/row*ed*

burs/ary
bury/*ing*
buse*s*
bushel
busily
busi/ness
bustl*ed*
busy
butane
but/chery
butte
butt*ed*
but/tock
button*ed*
but/tress*ed*
buxom
buy*er*
buz/zard
by
bye
by-law *also* bye-
   law

C

cabal/*istic*
cab/aret
cab/bage
cab/in*et*
cabri/olet
cach*ed*
cacophon/ous*ly*
cactus [cacti]
cadaver/ous*ly*
cad/die*d*
ca/dence

cadet/*ship*
cadre
Caesar/*ean also*
   Caesar/*ian*
caes/ura
café
cafet/eria
caf/feine
caftan
cagey
cahoot*s*
ca/jole*ry*
cala/bash
calamine
calamit/ous*ly*
calci/ferous
cal/cium
calcul/able
calcu/lator
Caledo/nian
calen/dar
calib/rate*d*
cal/ibration
cal/ibre
cal/ico*es*
caliph
calix [ca/lices]
calli/graphy
calli/pers *also*
   cal/ipers
callisthenics
   also cal/
   isthenics
cal/lous/*ness*
callus*es*
calm/*ness*
cal/orie

calor/ific
cal/umny
calx
calyp/sos
calyx*es also*
   calyces
camara/derie
cam/bric
camel
camel/lia
cameo*s*
cam/era
camou/flage*d*
cam/paigne*d*
campano/logy
camphor/ate*d*
Cana/dian
canal/ize*d*
ca/nary
can/cel*led*
cancer/*ous*
cande/labra
candes/cent
candida/ture
can/did*ly*
cand/our
canine
canis/ter
canker/*ous*
canna/bis
can/*nery*
cannibal/*istic*
cannon/ade
canoe/*ing*
canon/ize
canopy
cantanker/ous

can/tata
can/teen
canti/lever
canto*s*
can/vase*s* **n**
can/vass/*ing* **v**
can/yon
cap/abil/ity
capa/cious/*ness*
capacit/ance
capa/city
capil/lary
capital/*ism*
cap/itol
capon/*ize*
ca/price
capri/cious*ly*
cap/sicum
cap/size*d*
cap/sule
cap/tain*cy*
cap/tion
cap/tious*ly*
captiv/ate*d*
cara/mel
carat
caravan/*serai*
cara/way
carbo/hydrate
car/bolic
car/bon*a*/*ceous*
carbon/*ate*
carbon/*ifer*/*ous*
carbor/undum
carbur/et*tor*
car/cass *also*
   car/case

carcino/gen*ic*
car/diac
cardi/gan
car/dinal
cardio/graph*er*
ca/reene*d*
career/*ist*
care/ful/*ness*
care/less
caress*ed*
caret
car/goes
Carib/*bean*
cari/bou
carica/ture*d*
car/ies
car/mine
carna/tion
carni/val
carnivor/ous*ly*
carol*led*
ca/rotid
carou/sal
carou/sel
carpenter
carpentry
car/riag/*able*
car/rier
car/rion
carrot
carry/*ing*
cartel
cartil/age
carton
cartoon/*ist*
cart/ridge
cas/cade*d*

cas/cara
ca/sein
cashew
cash/ier*ed*
cash/mere
casi/no*s*
cas/sava
casser/ole
cas/sette
cas/sock
casso/wary
cast
casta/net
caste
cas/tigat*ed*
Cas/tilian
castor
cas/trat*ed*
casu/al*ty*
cata/bol/ism
cata/clysm*ic*
cata/comb
cata/lectic
cata/lepsy
cata/log *also*
   cata/logue
cata/lyst
cata/lytic
cata/maran
cata/pult*ed*
catar/act
catar/rh*al*
cata/strophe
catech/ism
category
cater*ed*
cater/pillar

cater/waul*ed*
cath/arsis
cathed/ral
cath/ode
catholi/*cism* (C)
Cau/casian
caucus*es*
caught
caul/dron
cauli/flower
caulk*ing*
caus/al*ly*
caustic/*ally*
cauter/iz*ed*
caution/*ary*
cautio*us*
caval/cade
cava/lier
cav/alry
cavern/*ous*
cavi/are
cavill*ed*
cav/ity
ca/vort*ed*
cay/enne
cease/*less*
cedar
ced*ed*
ceil/*ing*
celeb/rat*ed*
celeb/rity
celer/ity
celery
celesti/al*ly*
celib/ate
cel/lar*er*
cello/phane

cello*s*
cellu/*lar*
cellu/*loid*
cellu/*lose*
cement*ed*
cemet/ery
ceno/taph
censer
censor
censori/*ous*
cen/sur*ed*
cen/sus*es*
cental
cen/taur
centenar/ian
cent/ennial
centi/grade
centi/gramme
centi/litre
centi/metre
centi/pede
central/iz*ed*
centr*ed*
cent/ring
centri/fugal
centri/petal
centur/ion
cen/tury
ce/ramic
cereal
cerebel/lum
cereb/ral
ceremoni/ous*ly*
cere/mony
cerise
cer/taint*y*
certific/at*ed*

certi/tude
ceru/lean
cessa/tion
ces/sion
ceta/cean
chag/rin*ed*
chaise
chalet
chal/ic*ed*
chal/leng*ed*
chamber/*lain*
cha/meleon
cham/ois
cham/pagne
cham/pion*ed*
chan/cel/lery
chan/cel/lor
chan/cery
chan/delier
change/*able*
changing
chan/nell*ed*
chanti/cleer
chaos
cha/otic
chapel
chap/eron*ed*
chap/lainc*y*
character/*istic*
charade
charge/*able*
chariot/*eer*
charit/able
char/latan
char/treuse
chary
chasm*s*

chas/sis **s/p**
chastened
chastise/ment
chas/uble
chat/eau [eaux]
chat/tel
chauf/feur
chauvin/ism
checked
ched/dar
cheese
chee/tah
chemic/ally
chem/istry
che/nille
cheque
chequered
cher/ubim or
  cher/ubs
cheva/lier
chev/ron
chic
chi/canery
chicle
chic/ory
chief/tain
chif/fon
chil/blainy
chil/dren
chillies
chil/lier
chilly
chi/mera
chimer/ical
chim/neys
chimpan/zee

Chi/nese
chintz
chip/munk
chiro/podist
chiro/practic
chir/ruped
chiselled
chival/rously
chlor/ate
chlorin/ated
chlor/ine
chloro/formed
chloro/phyll
choc/olate
choice
choir
cholera
chol/eric
chook
choose
choosy
chop-suey
choral
chor/ale
chord
choreo/grapher
choric
choris/ter
chorused
chose
chough
christened
Christi/an/ity
Christ/mas
chro/matic
chrome
chro/mium

chromo/some
chron/icler
chrono/logical
chrono/meter
chrysa/lises or
  chrys/al/ides
chrys/
  anthemum
chuck/led
churl/ish/ness
churned
chute
chut/ney
ciao
cicada
cica/trice also
  cica/trix [ices]
cider
cigar/ette
cili/ated
cinched
cinder
cine/matic
ciner/aria
cinna/bar
cinna/mon
ciphered also
  cyphered
circ/let
circuit/ously
cir/cuits
circular/ity
circu/latory
circum/cized
circum/ference
circum/locu/tory
circum/scribed

circum/stan/tial
cir/cuses
cir/rhosis
cir/rous **a**
cirrus **n**
cissy or sissy
cis/tern
cit/adel
cited
citi/zenry
cit/ric
cit/ron
citrus
civet
civic/ally
civil/ian
civil/ity
clair/voyant
clam/oured
clamor/ously
clan/nish
claret
clari/fica/tion
clari/fying
clarinet/tist
classi/cism
classicist
classifi/able
clause
claustro/phobia
clavi/chord
clav/icle
clayey
cleanli/ness
clean/ness
cleansed
clear/ance

cleav/age
cleav*er*
cle*fs*
clem/*ency*
clere/story
clergy/*man*
cler/ic*al*
cleric/al*ly*
clerk
clich*és*
clien/t*ele*
climac/teric
cli/mactic
cli/matic
climax
climb
clime
clin/ic*al*
clique*s*
cliquish/*ness*
clois/ter*ed*
clos/et*ed*
closure
cloth*ed*
clothes
cloth*s*
clout
cloy*ed*
clue/*less*
clum/sily
clut/ter*ed*
coache*s*
co/adjutor
coagu/lat*ed*
co/alesc*ed*
coali/tion
coarse*ly*

coax*ed*
co/axial
co/balt*ic*
cobra
co/caine
coc/cygeal
coccyx
coch/ineal
coch/lea
cock/*erel*
cock/neys
cock/roache*s*
cocoa
coco/nut
co/coon
cod/eine
codi/cil
codi/fica/tion
cods/wallop
coef/ficient
coel/acanth
co/erc*ed*
co/ercible
co/eval*ly*
cof/fee
cof/fin*ed*
co/gent*ly*
cogit/at*ed*
cognac
cogniz/*ance*
cognit/ive
cognos/cente
coher/*ence*
co/hesion
co/horts
coif/fure
coin/*age*

co/incid/*ence*
coir
col/ander
colic
col/itis
col/labor/ator
col/lage
collaps/ible
collar/*ette*
collat/eral
col/league
col/lector
col/legi/ate
col/lid*ed*
colli/ery
col/linear
collision
col/loid*al*
col/loquial/*ism*
col/loquy [ies]
collu/sion
colon
col/onel
colo/nial
colon/ies
colon/nade
colo/phony
colori/meter
colos/sal
col/ossus*es or*
   co/lossi
colour/ful*ly*
colum/n*ar*
coma/*tose*
comb
com/bat*ed*
combat/*ant*

combust/*ible*
co/median
comedi/*enne*
comedy
comfort/*ably*
comic/al*ly*
coming
com/intern
comma
command/*ant*
com/mando*s*
com/memor/
   ated
com/mence/
   ment
commend/*able*
com/mensur/ate
comment/*ary*
comment/ator
com/mer/cial*ly*
com/miser/at*ed*
commis/sari*at*
com/mission/
   aire
commit/*ment*
commit/*tal*
com/mit*ted*
commit/tee
commodi/ous*ly*
commod/ity
common/*ness*
common/*wealth*
com/motion
commun/al*ly*
com/mun*ed*
com/munic/able
com/munion/*ist*

com/muniqué
commun/*ism*
com/mutat/*ive*
com/mut/*ator*
com/mut*er*
com/panion/
   able
compar/*able*
com/parat/*ively*
com/par*ed*
compar/*ison*
com/pass*es*
com/passion/*ate*
compat/*ibil/ity*
compat/*ible*
com/pel*led*
com/pendium
com/pens/*ating*
com/pensat/*ory*
compère
com/pet*ed*
com/petence
com/petit/*ively*
com/petitor
com/pil*er*
com/placency
com/plaisance
com/plement/
   ary
com/plet*ed*
com/plexion
com/plex/*ity*
com/pliance
complic/*ated*
com/plicity
compliment/*ary*
comply/*ing*

com/ponent
compos/*itely*
com/pos/*itor*
com/posure
com/pote
com/pound
comprehens/*ible*
comprehen/*sion*
comprehens/*ive*
compress/*ible*
com/press*or*
comprom/*ised*
compuls/*ory*
com/punction
com/puter
com/rad*ely*
con/cave
con/ceal*ed*
con/ced*ed*
con/ceit*ed*
con/ceivable
concen/trate
concentra/*tion*
con/centri/*city*
con/ceptual/*ism*
con/cern*ed*
concer/*tina*
con/certos
con/cession
concho/logy
con/cil/iar
con/ciliat/*ory*
con/cisely
con/cluded
conclus/*ively*
con/coct*ion*
con/comit/*ance*

concord/*ance*
con/course
con/cretely
concu/bine
con/cupis/cence
concur/*rence*
concus/*sion*
con/cyc/lic
condem/*natory*
con/dens*er*
con/descen/sion
con/dign
condi/ment
con/dition/*ally*
con/dolence
condom
con/domin/ium
con/don*ed*
condor
conduc/ible
con/ducive
con/duct*or*
con/duct*ress*
con/duit
con/fection/*ery*
con/feder/ate
confer/*ence*
con/fer*red*
con/fess*or*
con/fetti
confid/ant
con/fiden/*tial*
con/figura/*tion*
confirma/*tion*
con/fiscat/*ory*
con/flagra/*tion*
con/flict

con/fluence
conform/*able*
conforma/*tion*
con/fronta/*tion*
con/fusion
con/geal*ed*
con/genial
con/genit/*ally*
con/gest*ed*
con/glomer/ate
con/gratu/lat/
   ory
con/grega/tion
congres/*sional*
con/gruency
con/gruent
conic/*ally*
con/ifer/*ous*
con/jec/tural
conjug/*ally*
con/juga/tion
conjunct/*ive*
con/jurer (or)
connect/*ible*
con/nection
con/ned
con/nivance
connois/seur
con/nota/tion
con/nubial
con/queror
con/san/guin/
   eous
con/science
con/scien/tious
con/scious/*ness*
con/scription

con/secrated
con/secut/ive*ly*
con/sensus
con/sent*ed*
con/sequen/t*ial*
con/servat/ive
con/servat/ory
con/sider/*able*
con/sidera/*tion*
con/sign*or*
consist/ent*ly*
con/sistor/ial
con/solat/ory
con/sol*ed*
con/solid/at*ed*
con/sommé
conson/ance
conson/ant
con/sort*ium*
con/spicu/ous*ly*
conspir/acy
con/spirator/*ial*
con/stable
con/stabul/ary
con/stancy
constella/tion
consterna/tion
constip/at*ed*
con/stitu/ency
con/sti/tut*es*
con/stitu/tion*al*
con/strict*or*
con/struct/*ive*
con/struct*or*
con/stru*ed*
con/substanti/
    ate

consul*ar*
con/sult/*ant*
consum/mate
con/sumption
con/tact*ed*
con/tagious*ly*
con/tamina/tion
con/temn*ed*
con/templat/ive
con/temporan/
    eous
con/tempor/ary
contempt/*ible*
con/temptu/*ous*
con/ten/tion
con/ten/tious*ly*
contermin/ous
contest/*ant*
con/textu/al*ly*
con/tigu/ous
contin/ent*al*
contin/gency
con/tinu/ance
con/tinu/ity
con/tinu/ous*ly*
con/tinuum
con/tortion/*ist*
con/tour*ed*
contra/band
contra/cept/ive
con/tractor*
contractu/al*ly*
contra/dict*ory*
con/tralt*os*
con/traption
contra/puntal
contrari/ety

con/trar/ily
contra/ven*ed*
contrib/utory
con/trite*ly*
con/trivance
con/troll*ed*
control/*ler*
contro/versial*ly*
contro/versy
con/tumely
con/tusion
conun/drum
conval/esc*ence*
con/veni/*ence*
con/venticle
con/vention/al*ly*
con/verg*ence*
con/versant
con/versa/tion*al*
con/vers*ed*
con/version
convert/*ible*
convex/*ity*
convey/*ancer*
con/vict*ion*
con/vincible
conviv/ial*ly*
con/voc/ation
con/vok*ed*
con/volut*ed*
con/vol/vulus
con/voy*ed*
con/vuls*ed*
co/n(e)ys *also*
    conies
coolie *also*
    cooly

cool*ly*
co-operative
co-operator
co-opt*ed*
co-ordinator
co/peck, *also* ko/
    peck, ko/pec
copi/ous*ly*
copu/lat/ive
coquet*ry*
coquette
cor/acle
coral
coral/*line*
cord
cordial/*ity*
cor/don*ed*
cor/duroy
core
co-respondent
cormor/ant
cor/neal
cor/nelian *also*
    car/nelian
cornet
cor/nice
cornu/copia
co/rolla
corol/lary
coron/a*ry*
cor/ona/tion
cor/oner
corpor/al*ly*
cor/pora/tion
corpor/eal
corps
corpse

corpu/lent
cor/puscle
cor/ralled
cor/rector
correl/ated
cor/respond/
  ence
cor/ridor
corri/gendum
cor/rigible
cor/robor/ated
cor/roboree
cor/roded
corros/ive
corrug/ated
corrupt/ible
cors/age
cor/seted
cortis/one
corus/cated
cor/vette
co-signatory
cosine
cos/metic/ally
cosmic/ally
cosmog/ony
cosmo/politan
cosmos
Cos/sack
cos/seted
cos/tume
cos/tumier also
  cos/tumer
cosy
co/tan/gent
co/terie
cotermin/ous

cot/tager
cot/ter
cot/toned
coty/ledon/ous
cougar
coughed
cou/lomb
coun/cillor
coun/sellor
counten/anced
counter/feiter
counter/pane
coun/tries
county
coup de grâce
coup d'état
couplet
coupling
cou/pon
courage/ously
cour/ier
course
court
cour/teously
cour/tesan
cour/tesy
court/ier
cousin
coutur/ier m
cou/turi/ère f
cov/enanter
cover/age
cov/ertly
coveted
covetous/ness
coveys
coward/ice

cowrie (cowry)
cox/swain
coy/ly
coyote
cra/nial
cra/nium
cranny
crated
crater
cra/vatted
craven/ness
crayoned
crazy
creaked
creased
cre/atively
cre/ator
crea/ture
crèche
creden/tials
cred/ible
credit/able
cred/itor
credos
creed
creek
cre/mated
cremator/ium
crenel/lated
cre/ole (C)
creo/soted
crêpe
crepit/ated
crepus/cular
cres/cendos
cres/cent
cretin/ous

cre/tonne
cre/vasse
crev/ice
crick/eter
crier
crime passionel
criminal/ity
crim/soned
cringing
crinkly
crip/pled
crisis [crises]
cri/terion [ia]
criti/cism
criti/cize
cri/tique
cro/cheted
crock/ery
croco/dile
cro/cuses
crony [ies]
cro/quet
cro/quette
crot/chety
crouched
croup
crou/pier
cru/cial
cru/cible
cruci/fixion
cruci/form
cruelly
cruelty
cruet
cruiser
cru/sader
cruse

18

crus/tacean
cryptic
crypto/gram
crystal/*line*
crystal/lized
cu/bical
cu/bicle
cubism
cuckoo
cucum/ber
cud/gel*led*
cu*ed*
cuis/ine
cul-/de-/sac
culin/ary
culmin/at*ed*
culp/able
cul/prit
cul/tiv/able
cultiv/ator
cul/tural
cul/vert
cummer/bund
cum/quat
cumu/lat/ive
cumul/ous **a**
cu/mulus **n**
cunei/form
cup/board
cup/*ful*
cupid/ity
cu/pola
cur/able
cura/çao *also*
  cura/çoa
curare
cur/ate

cur/ator
curb ↔ kerb **n**
curb*ed* **v**
curdl*ed*
cur/ett*ed*
cur/few
curio*s*
curi/osity
curi/ous*ly*
cur/lew
cur/mudgeon
cur/rant
cur/rency
cur/rent
curric/ulum
curs/ive
curs/ory
cur/tail*ed*
cur/tain*ed*
curtsied *also*
  curtsey*ed*
curtsy/*ing also*
  curtsey/*ing*
curva/ture
cur/vett*ed also*
  curvet*ed*
curvi/linear
cush/ion*ed*
cusp/idor
custard
cus/todian
custom/*ary*
cus/tom*er*
cuta/neous
cut/icle
cut/lass*es*
cut/lery

cyan/ide
cyber/netics
cycad
cyc/lamen
cycl*ed*
cyc/lic*al*
cyc/lone
cyc/lo/paedia
cyclo/style
cyclo/tron
cygnet*s*
cylin/der
cylin/drical
cym/bal
cyn/ic*al*
cynos/ure
cypher*ed also*
  cipher*ed*
cy/press*es*
Cyril/lic
cyst
cyto/logy
czar *also* tsar
Czecho/*slovak*

D

dachs/hund
daffo/dil
daguerre/otype
dahlia
daily
dai/quiri
daises
dalli/ance
dally/*ing*

Dal/matia*n*
dam/ag*ed*
damask
dam*med*
damna/*tion*
damn*ed*
damsel
damson
dan/delion
dan/druff
danger/*ous*
Danish
daphne
Darwin/*ian*
data
daub*ed*
daugh/ter
daunt/*less*
dawd/l*ed*
dazzl*ed*
deacon/*ess*
dead/en*ed*
deadli/*ness*
dead/*lock*
deaf/en*ed*
dean/*ery*
dear
dearth
de/bar*red*
de/bas*ed*
de/batable
de/bauch*ed*
deben/ture
debilit/at*ed*
deb/it*ed*
debon/air
de/bouch*ed*

debris
debtor
de/bug/ging
decade
decad/ence
deca/gonal
deca/logue (D)
de/canter
de/capit/ated
de/carbon/ized
de/cayed
de/ceased
deceit/fully
de/ceived
de/celer/ated
Decem/ber
de/cency
decent
de/central/ized
decept/ively
deci/bel
de/cided
de/cidu/ously
deci/litre
decimal/iza/tion
deci/metre
de/ciphered
de/cision
de/cis/ively
de/clama/tion
de/clamat/ory
de/clara/tion
de/clared
de/clen/sion
de/clina/tion
decliv/ity
de/com/posed

de/con/tamin/
   ated
décor
decor/ator
decor/ously
de/corum
decoys
de/creased
de/creed
decre/ment
de/crepit/ude
dedic/atory
de/duction
deemed
deer
de/famat/ory
de/faulter
de/feat/ism
de/fec/ated
de/fect/ive
de/fence
defend/ant
defens/ible
defer/ence
de/ferred
de/fiantly
de/fi/ciency
de/fi/cit
defied
defin/itely
defini/tion
de/flection
de/frauded
de/frayed
deftly
de/funct

defy/ing
de/gener/acy
de/grada/tion
de/hyd/rated
deify/ing
deigned
deity [de/ities]
de/lect/able
deleg/ated
de/leted
dele/teri/ously
delft
de/liber/ately
del/icacy
deli/ca/tes/sen
deli/ciously
de/lineated
de/lin/quency
de/liques/cent
de/liri/ously
de/lirium
de/liver/ance
del/taic
de/luded
de/luged
delu/sion
dem/agoguery
de/marca/tion
de/mean
demean/our
de/men/tia
de/mesne
demise
de/mobil/ized
demo/cracy
demo/cratic
demo/graphy

de/mol/ished
de/moli/tion
demoni/acal
demon/strable
demon/strat/ive
demon/strator
de/murely
demur/rage
de/murred
demur/rer
de/nial
denied
denig/rated
denim
de/nitri/fy/ing
den/izen
de/nomina/
   tional
de/nomin/ator
dé/noue/ment
densely
dens/ity
dent/ally
denti/frice
den/tures
de/nuda/tion
de/nunci/ation
deny/ing
de/odor/ant
de/odor/ized
de/parture
de/pend/able
de/pend/ants n
de/pend/ence n
de/pend/ent a
de/pictor
de/pleted

de/ployed
de/polar/ized
de/ponent
de/pos/itor
depot
de/prav/ity
de/prec/ated
de/preci/ated
de/preda/tion
de/press/ant
de/priva/tion
depth
depu/tized
de/rail/ment
derel/iction
de/rision
de/ris/ory
de/riva/tion
de/riv/at/ive
derma/titis
derogat/ory
der/rick
der/vish
descend/ant
des/cent
de/scribed
de/scrip/tion
desec/rated
de/segreg/ated
de/sensit/ized
des/ert n/v
de/serted
dés/habillé
de/sic/cator
desid/er/atum
  [ta]
de/signer

desir/able
de/sirous
de/sisted
desol/ately
des/paired
de/spatched use
  dis/patched
desper/adoes
des/per/ately
despic/able
des/pised
des/potic
des/sert n
des/tiny
des/troyer
destruct/ible
desul/tory
detach/able
detach/ment
detect/ive
de/tector
dé/tente
de/tergent
deterior/ated
determina/tion
deter/mine
de/ter/rent
detest/able
deton/ator
detour
de/tribal/ize
detri/ment/ally
de/tritus
deuce
Deutero/nomy

devast/ated
de/veloped
develop/mental
de/vi/ation
device n
devil/led
devil/ry
de/vised
devoid
de/voted
de/voured
de/voutly
dexter/ity
dex/tr/ously
dhow
dia/betes
dia/bolic/ally
dia/crit/ical
diadem
di/aer/esis [eses]
dia/gnosed
dia/gnosis [oses]
diagon/ally
dia/gram/matic
dia/lectic/ally
di/alled
dia/logues
diamanté
dia/meter
dia/metric/ally
dia/mond
dia/pason
diaper
dia/phan/ous
dia/phragmatic
diar/ist
dia/rrhoea

diary
dia/spora
dia/stole
dia/thermy
dice
di/chlor/ide
dicho/tomy
di/chromate
dicoty/ledon/ous
dictat/or/ial
diction/ary
didacti/cism
didger/idoo
di/elec/tric
die [dice] n
diesel
diet/ary
diet/etic/ally
dietitian also
  dietician
dif/fered
dif/fer/ence
dif/feren/tially
dif/ficulty
dif/fi/dently
dif/fraction
dif/fusion
digest/ible
digest/ive
di/gital
digni/fying
dignit/ary
di/gres/sion
dike
dilapid/ated
di/lated
dilat/ory

di/lemma
dilet/tante
dili/gence
dilu/tion
dimen/sion*al*
di/meter
dimin/ish*ed*
di/minut/*ively*
dim/ity
din*ed*
dinghy
dingo*es*
dingy
dining-/room
dinkum
dinner-/table
dino/saur/*ian*
dio/cesan
dio/cese
diode
diph/theria
diph/thong
dip/lomae*d*
diplo/mat*ic*
di/polar
dire
direct/*ive*
director/*ate*
direct/*ory*
dirge
diri/gible
dirndl
dis/advant/
  age/*ous*
dis/agree/*able*
dis/allow*ed*
dis/appear/*ance*

dis/ap/point*ed*
dis/approval
dis/array*ed*
dis/aster
disast/r*ously*
dis/belief
dis/believ*ed*
dis/burse/*ment*
disc *also* disk
dis/cern/*ment*
dis/ciple
disciplin/ary
discip/lin*ed*
dis/closure
dis/coloura/*tion*
dis/comfit*ed*
dis/comfort*ed*
dis/composure
dis/concert*ed*
dis/connect*ed*
dis/consol/ate*ly*
dis/continu/*ous*
dis/cord/ant*ly*
disco/thèque
dis/count/*able*
dis/courag*ed*
dis/cours*ed*
dis/courteous
dis/courtesy
dis/covery
dis/credit/*able*
dis/creet
dis/crep/ancy
dis/crete
dis/cretion
dis/crimin/at/*ory*
dis/curs/ive*ly*

discus
dis/cuss*ed*
discus/sion
disdain/ful*ly*
dis/eas*ed*
dis/embarka/
  tion
dis/embodied
dis/embowell*ed*
dis/figur/ation
dis/gorg*ed*
dis/grace/ful*ly*
dis/gruntl*ed*
dis/guis*ed*
dis/gust*ed*
dis/habille
dis/hearten*ed*
dish/evell*ed*
dis/honesty
dis/honour/*able*
dis/illusion*ed*
dis/infect/*ant*
dis/ingenu/*ously*
dis/inher/it*ed*
dis/integ/rat*ed*
dis/inter/est*ed*
dis/inter/r*ed*
disk *also* disc
dis/mal*ly*
dis/may*ed*
dis/miss*al*
dis/obedi/ence
dis/obey*ed*
dis/organ/iz*ed*
dis/parag*ed*
dis/parate*ly*
dis/par/ity

dis/passion/ate*ly*
dis/patch*ed*
dis/pell*ed*
dispens/able
dispens/ary
dis/pens*ed*
dis/pers*ed*
disper/sion
dis/pirit*ed*
dis/pleasure
dis/port*ed*
dis/posable
dis/posal
dis/posi/tion
dis/possess
dis/proportion/
  ate*ly*
dis/putable
dis/quali/fy*ing*
dis/reput/able
dis/respect/ful*ly*
dis/rup*tion*
dis/satis/faction
dis/satis/fied
dis/satisfy
dis/sector
dis/sembl*ed*
dis/semin/ate
dis/sension
dis/sent*er*
dis/senti*ent*
dis/service
dissid/ent
dis/similar
dis/simu/lat*ed*
dissip/at*ed*
dis/soci/at*ed*

dissol/ute*ly*
dis/solu/tion
dis/solv*ed*
dis/sonance **n**
dis/sonant **a**
dis/suad*ed*
dissyl/lable *also*
  disyl/lable
dis/taff
dis/tance*d*
dis/taste/*ful*
dis/temper
dis/tend*ed*
distil/*late*
dis/till*ed*
dis/tinc*tion*
dis/tinguish*ed*
dis/tor*tion*
dis/trac*tion*
dis/traught
distribu/tion
distribu/tive
dis/trict
disturb/*ance*
dis/unity
dis/use
disyl/lable *also*
  dissyl/lable
dithy/ramb*ic*
ditto*s*
ditty [ies]
diurn/al*ly*
div/ag/ate*d*
divan
di/varic/ate*d*
di/vergen*t*
di/verse

di/versi/fy/*ing*
di/vers/ity
di/vest*ed*
div/id*ed*
divi/dend
divine*ly*
divin/ity
divis/ibil/ity
divi/sion
di/visor
di/vorce*e*
divot
di/vulg*ed*
dizzi/ness
do/cile*ly*
dock/et*ed*
doctor/*ate*
doctrin/aire
doc/trinal
doc/trine
docu/ment/*ary*
dod/dery
dodo(*e*)s
doe
does*n't*
dogg*ed*
dog/gerel
dog/ma*tic*
dol/drums
dole/ful*ly*
dollar
dolo/mite
dol/or/ous*ly*
dol/phin
do/main
domest/ic*ity*
domin/an*t*

domin/eer*ed*
domin/oes
donate
don/*nish*
donor
dorm/ant
dormit/ory
dorsal
dosage
dose
dos/sier
dotage
dotard
dot*ed*
doub/ling
doub/loon
doubtful*ly*
douch*ed*
dough
doughty
dous*ed* ↔
  dows*ed*
dow/ager
dowel/*ling*
downy
dowry
dows*ed* ↔
  dous*ed*
doxo/logy
doyen
doyley *also*
  doily
doz*ed*
drachma*s*
  [chmae]
drafts/man
dragon

dra/goon*ed*
drain/*age*
dram*at*/*ist*
draper*y*
drastic/*ally*
draughts/man
draughts/
  man/*ship*
draughty
drawe*r*
drawl*ed*
dread/ful*ly*
dread/nought
dreari/est
dreary
dreg*s*
drlb/let
drily *also* dryly
drip/*ping*
drivel/*ling*
drizzly
droll/*ery*
dromed/ary
dron*ed*
drool*ed*
droop*ed*
drop*ped*
drought
drows*ed*
drowsy
drub/*bing*
drudg*ed*
drug/*gist*
drunken/*ness*
dryad
dryly *also* drily
dual ↔ duel

dubi/ously
ducal
ducat
duch/ess
duchy
duct/ile
dudgeon
due
duel/list
duet/tist
duffle *also* duffel
dugong
dulcet
dulci/mer
dull/ness
dully
duly
duma
dumb/found
dune
dungar/ees
dun/geon
dunn/age
dunned
duo/decimal
duo/denum
duo/logue
duplic/ator
dupli/city
durable
durance
duress
du/teously
duti/able
duti/ful
dwarf/ish
dwell/ing

dwindled
dye/ing
dying
dyke *use* dike
dynam/ical
dynam/ited
dyna/mos
dynasty [ies]
dyne
dys/entery
dys/pepsia

E

eagerly
eaglet
ear/ful
earn/estly
earn/ings
earthen/ware
earth/quake
ease/ful
easel
eas/ily
Easter
east/erly
east/ern
eaves
ebbed
ebony
ebulli/ent
ebulli/tion
ec/centri/city
ec/clesi/astic
echelon
ech/idnas

echoes
éclair
ec/lect/icism
eclipsed
eco/logy
eco/nomic/ally
ec/stas/ized
ec/stasy
ecumen/ical
eczema
edel/weiss
edging
edgy
edible
edict
edi/fice
edi/fying
editor/ial
edu/cator
eerie
eer/ily
ef/faced
effect/ive
effec/tive/ness
ef/fectual
ef/femin/ate
ef/fervescent
effete
effi/ca/ciously
effi/ciency
effi/ciently
effigy [ies]
ef/florescence
ef/fluent
ef/fluvium [via]
ef/fluxion
effort/lessly

effront/ery
ef/fusively
egalit/ar/ian
eglan/tine
ego/centric
egot/ism
egre/giously
egres/sion
egret
Egyp/tian
eider/down
eighth
eighti/eth
eistedd/fod
ejacu/lated
ejector
eked
elabor/ated
élan
eland
elapsed
elasti/city
elated
el/bowed
eld/erly
eld/est
election/eered
elector/ate
electric/ally
electri/cian
electri/city
electro/cu/tion
elec/trode
electro/lys/ing
electro/lysis
electro/lytic
elec/tronic

eleg/ant*ly*
ele/giac
elegy
element/*ary*
elephanti/*asis*
eleva/tion
elev/ator
elev/en*th*
elf*in*
eli/cit*ed*
eli/gible
elimin/ator
elision
ellipt/ic*al*
elocu/tion/*ary*
elonga/tion
elo/quence
elucid/atory
elud*ed*
elus/ive*ly*
emaci/at*ed*
eman/at*ed*
emancipa/tion
eman/cip/ist
emascu/lat*ed*
embalm/*ment*
em/bargo*es*
em/bark*a*/tion
em/barrass/*ment*
em/bassy
em/bed*ded* also
  imbedd*ed*
em/bellish/*ment*
embers

em/bezzle/*ment*
emblemat/ic*al*
em/bodi/ment
em/bol/ism
em/boss*ed*
em/brace/*able*
em/brasure
em/broca/tion
em/broid/ery
em/bry/o*nic*
em/bryo*s*
emend/*ator*
emerald/*ine*
emer/gency
emer/itus
emery
emetic
emig/rat*ed*
émigré
emin/ence
emir
emis/sary
emis/sion
emitt*ed*
emol/lient
emolu/ment
emotion/al*ly*
emo/tive
em/panel*led*
  also im/
  panel*led*
em/pathy
em/peror
em/phasis
emphas/iz*ed*
em/pire
empir/ic*al*

em/ploy*ee*
em/ploy*er*
empor/ium
emp/ress
emp/tied
em/pyrean
emu/lat*ed*
emulsi/fy*ing*
emul/sion
emu*s*
enabl*ed*
enamel*led*
en/amour*ed*
en/cephalo/gram
en/closure
en/compass*ed*
encor*ed*
en/counter*ed*
en/courage/*ment*
en/croach*ed*
en/cumbrance
en/cyclic*al*
en/cyclo/paedia
en/deav/our*ed*
en/demic/*ally*
endo/gamy
endo/morph
en/dorse/*ment*
  also in/
  dorse/*ment*
endow/*ment*
en/du*ed* also
  indu*ed*
en/durance
enema*s*
enemy
  [enemies]

ener/getic/*ally*
ener/giz*ed*
energy
ener/vat*ed*
enfi/lad*ed*
en/fold*ed* also
  infold*ed*
en/force/*able*
en/franch/is*ed*
en/gag/ingly
engin/*eer*
Eng/lish
en/gross*ed*
enig/matic*al*
en/large/*ment*
en/mity
en/noble*d*
ennui
enorm/ity
enorm/ous
enough
en/quire *also*
  inquire
enrol
en/roll*ed*
en route
en/sconc*ed*
en/semble
en/sign
en/su*ed*
en/sur*ed*
en/tail*ed*
en/teric
enter/prise
enter/tain/*ment*
en/thral
en/thrall*ed*

en/thusi/asm
entice/*ment*
entire*ly*
entity [ies]
entomb/*ment*
entomo/logy
entour/age
en/tranced
en/treaty
entrée
en/trenched
entre/preneur
en/tropy
enumer/ated
enunci/ated
envel/ope **n**
envelop/*ing*
envi/able
envi/ous*ly*
en/viron/*ment*
envis/aged
envoys
envy/*ing*
enzyme
epaul/ette
épée
eph/emeral
epicur/e*an*
epi/demic
epi/dermis
epi/gen/esis
epi/lepsy
epi/logue
episcopa/li*an*
epis/ode

epistle
epistol/ary
epi/taph
epi/thet
epi/tome
epoch
equ/able
equal/ized
equal/*ity*
equalled
equanim/ity
equa/tion
equat/or/*ial*
eques/trian **a/n**
equestri/enne
f/n
equi/distant
equi/lateral
equi/librium
equine
equi/noctial
equi/nox
equip/*ment*
equi/poise
equip/ped
equit/able
equi/val/ent
equivoc/al*ly*
era
eradic/ated
erasure
ere
erected
erg
ergo
ermine
eroded

ero/sion
erotic/*ally*
errand
er/rant*ry*
erratic/*ally*
erred
errone/ous*ly*
error
erudi/tion
erup*tion*
erysip/elas
escal/ade
escal/ator
escap/ade
escaped
es/capism
escarp/*ment*
eschato/logy
eschewed
escorted
escrit/oire
escutcheon also
    scutcheon
Eski/mos
eso/teric
espal/ier
espe/ci*ally*
espial
espion/age
esplan/ade
es/pousal
es/poused
es/presso
espy/*ing*
es/quire
essay/*ist*
es/sence

essen/tial*ly*
estab/lish/*ment*
esteemed
estim/able
estim/ated
estranged
estu/ary
et cetera
etch/*ing*
etern/al*ly*
etern/ity
ether/eal*ly*
ethic/al*ly*
ethnic/al*ly*
ethno/logical
ethos
eti/ology
eti/quette
etymo/logy
eu/calyptus
Euchar/ist
euchre
eu/genic
eu/logy [ies]
eunuch
euphem/ism
eu/phonium
eu/phony
eu/phoria
eu/phu/ism
eureka
eu/rhythmic
Euro/pe*an*
eu/thanasia
evacu/ated
evaded
evalu/ated

evanes/cent
evangelic/ally
evapor/ated
eva/sion
even/ness
eventu/ality
eventu/ally
evic/tion
evid/ence
evid/ently
evil/ly
eviscer/ated
evoca/tion
evoked
evolu/tion/ary
ewe
ewer
ex of/ficio
ex/acer/bated
exact/ly
ex/agger/ated
exalta/*tion*
examina/tion
ex/asper/ated
excav/ated
ex/ceeded
excel/*lence*
ex/celsior
ex/ceptional
ex/cerpt
excess/ively
exchange/*able*
ex/chequer
ex/cised
ex/citable
excite/*ment*
ex/citing/ly

ex/clama/tion
exclus/ively
ex/communic/
   ated
ex/cori/ated
excre/ment
ex/cres/cence
ex/creted
ex/cruci/ated
ex/culp/ated
excur/sion
ex/cursus [ses]
ex/cusable
ex/cuse **n/v**
ex/ecrable
execut/ive
exec/utor
exem/plary
ex/emption
exer/cise **n/v**
ex/ertion
ex/hala/tion
ex/haustion
exhib/itor
exhilar/ated
ex/horta/tion
exi/gency
exist/*ence*
existen/tial
exit
exodus
ex/orbit/antly
exor/cism
exor/cized
exotic/ally
ex/panse
ex/pans/ively

ex/pati/ated
ex/patri/ated
expect/antly
ex/pecta/tions
ex/pector/ated
expedi/ently
exped/ited
ex/pedi/tion/ary
ex/pedi/tiously
ex/pelled
expend/able
expend/*iture*
ex/penses
expens/ively
ex/peri/enced
ex/peri/en/tially
ex/peri/ment/
   ally
ex/pert/*ise*
expi/ated
expira/tion
ex/plana/tion
ex/planat/ory
ex/pletive
ex/plicit/ly
ex/ploded
ex/ploit/*able*
ex/plora/tion
explos/ive
ex/ponen/tial
ex/port/*able*
ex/posi/tion
ex/postu/latory
ex/posure
ex/pression/*ism*
express/ively
ex/propri/ated

ex/pul/sion
ex/punged
ex/purg/ated
exquis/itely
extant
ex/temporan/
   eous
ex/tempore
extend/*ible*
ex/tensor
ex/tenu/ation
exter/ior
ex/termin/ated
ex/ternal/ized
ex/tinction
exting/uisher
extlrp/ated
extol
ex/tolled
ex/tortion/ate
ex/tract/*able*
extradi/tion
extrane/ously
extra/ordin/ary
extra/pol/ated
extra/territ/
   orial/*ity*
extra/vag/ance
extravag/ant
extravag/anzas
ex/tremely
extrem/ity
ex/tric/ated
extro/version
extro/vert
ex/truded
ex/tru/sion

ex/uber/ant*ly*
exult/ant*ly*
eye/*let*
eyrie

F

fabled
fabric/ated
fab/ulous*ly*
façade
facet
fa/cetious*ly*
facial
facile*ly*
facil/it/ate
facil/ity
fac/simile
fac/titious*ly*
factor/ial*ly*
factory [ies]
factu/al*ly*
fad/*dish*
faeces
faggot
Fahren/heit
fail/*ure*
faint
fair
fait accom/pli
faith/full*ly*
fakir
fal/cone*r*
fal/lacious*ly*
fal/lacy
fall/ible

fallow
fal/setto*s*
fals/ity
faltere*d*
famili/ar/*ity*
famine
famishe*d*
fanatic/al*ly*
fanci/full*ly*
fancy/*ing*
fan/fare
fan/tasia
fant/asy *also*
    phan/tasy
farce
farcic/al*ly*
fare
far/rago*s*
far/rier
far*ther*
far*thest*
fascia
fascin/ating
Fas/cism
fashion/*able*
fastene*d*
fas/tidi/ous*ly*
fatal/*ity*
fathere*d*
fathome*d*
fa/tigue*d*
fa/tiguing
fat/uous*ly*
faucet
faulte*d*
faun
fauna

faux pas
favour/*able*
favour/*ite*
fawne*d*
feas/ibil/ity
feas/ible
feather/weight
fea/ture*d*
feb/rile
Febru/ary
fecund/*ity*
feder/al*ly*
federa/tion
fee
feel/ing*s*
feigne*d*
feinte*d*
feld/spar
felicit/ate*d*
feline
fel/latio
fel/low
felony
fel/spar *use* feld/
    spar
femin/ine
feminin/ity
fem/oral
femur
ferment/*able*
fero/cious*ly*
fero/city
ferrel
fer/rete*d*
ferric
fer/rous
fer/rule ↔ ferule

fertil/izer
ferule ↔ ferrule
fer/vent*ly*
fer/vour
festiv/ity
fes/toone*d*
fête*d*
fetid *also* foetid
fetish
fet/lock
fettere*d*
fetuses *use*
    foetuse*s*
feud/al*ly*
fever/ish*ly*
fiancé **m**
fiancée **f**
fias/co*s*
fibre
fibro/sitis
fib/rous
fib/ula*s*
fic/tion*al*
ficti/tious*ly*
fidel/ity
fidgete*d*
fields/*man*
fiend/ish*ly*
fierce*ly*
fiery
fiesta
fifth*ly*
fif/tieth
figurat/ive*ly*
fila/gree (lig)
fila/ment/*ary*
fili/al*ly*

28

fili/buster
fili/gree *also* fila/
   gree
filings
fil/le*ted*
fil/ling*s*
fil/lip
filly
film*y*
filter*ed*
filth/*ily*
fil/trate
finale
final/*ity*
finan/cial*ly*
finan/cier
fine/*ness*
fin/esse*d*
finick/ing
finis
finite*ly*
Finn
Finn/ish
fiord
firkin
firma/ment
fiscal
fission/*able*
fis/sure
fisti/cuffs
five-/eighths
fixat/*ive*
fix*ity*
fix/*ture*
fjord *use* fiord
flabber/gasted
flabbi/ness

flaccid/*ity*
flagel/lator
flagon
flag/rant*ly*
flail*ed*
flair
flaky
flam/beau*s*
   (aux)
flamboy/ant
flaming
flamin/goe*s*
flam/mable
flange
flannel/*ette*
flan/nel*led*
flare
flat/ter*y*
flatu/lent
flaunt*ed*
flaut/ist
flavour/*less*
flaw/less/*ness*
flax*en*
flay*ed*
fledge
fledge/ling *also*
   fledg/ling
fleecy
flex/*ible*
flex*ion*
flier *use* flyer
flimsy
flip/pant*ly*
float
floata/tion *use*
   flota/tion

floe
floral
flores/cence
florid/*ity*
florin
flor/ist
flo/tilla*s*
flounce*d*
flour/ish*ed*
floury
flout/*ing*
flower*y*
flu
fluctu/ate*d*
flue
flu/ency
fluid/*ity*
flum/mery
flun/key*s*
fluor/escence
fluorid/ate
fluor/ide
flur/ried
fluty
flu/vial
flux
flyer
foal*ed*
focal
fo'c's'le *also*
   forecastle
focus [foci] **n**
focus(*s*)*ed* **v**
fodder
foe*s*
foetid *also* fetid
foetus*es*

fogey *use* fogy
foggy
foible
foist*ed*
foli/age
folio*s*
folk/lore
foll/icle
fomenta/*tion*
fond/ant
fontan/elle
fool/*ery*
for/aging
foray*s*
for/bade *also*
   for/bad
for/bear ↔ fore/
   bear
forbid/*den*
force/ful*ly*
forceps
for/cibly
fore
fore/arm*ed*
fore/bear*s* ↔
   for/bear
fore/boding
fore/caster
fore/castle *also*
   fo'c's'le
fore/close*d*
fore/fathers
fore/foot
fore/gather *also*
   for/gather
forego ↔ forgo
fore/hand

fore/head
for/eigner
fore/lock
fore/man
fore/most
for/ensic
fore/see
fore/shore
fore/sight
fore/skin
fore/stall
for/estry
fore/taste
fore/tell
fore/thought
fore/warned
fore/woman
fore/word
for/feited
forfeit/ure
for/gather
forgery
forget/ting
forgive/ness
forgo ↔ forego
for/lorn/ness
formal/ity
format
formid/able
fornica/tion
for/sake
forte
forth
forth/coming
forth/rightly
forth/with
forti/eth

forti/fying
fort/ress
fortuit/ously
fortu/nately
forty
forum
for/warded
fos/sicked
fossil/ized
foully
foundered
foundry [ies]
foun/tain
four/teen
fourthly
fowl
foyer
fracas
frac/tional
frac/tiously
frac/tured
fra/gilely
fragil/ity
fragment/ary
fra/grantly
frailty
franc
franch/ise
frangi/pane
frangi/pani
frank/furter
frank/incense
frantic/ally
frappé
fratern/ity
fratern/ized
fraudu/lently

fraught
fräu/lein
frayed
freak/ishly
free/dom
free/sia
freezing
freighter
frenetic also
      phrenetic
frenzy
frequen/cies
fre/quency
fre/quently
fresco(e)s
fret/ted
Freud/ian
friary
fricas/see
fricat/ive
fric/tional
fridge
friendli/ness
frier use fryer
Frie/sian
frieze
frig/ate
fright/fully
frigid/ity
fringe
fringing
frisk/ily
frit/tered
frivol/ously
frizzled
frolick/ing
frolic/some

frond
front/age
front/ally
fron/tier
frontis/piece
frowzy
fruct/ifying
frugal/ity
fruit/erer
fru/ition
frus/trated
fryer
fuch/sia
fuelled
fugit/ive
fugue
ful/crum
ful/fil
ful/filled
fulfil/ment
full
fulmin/ated
ful/ness use
      full/ness
ful/somely
fumig/ated
functional
function/ary
funda/mental
funeral n
funer/eal a
fung/ous a
fungus n
funicu/lar
fun/nelled
fun/nily
fur/bished

furi/ous*ly*
fur/long
fur/nace
fur/nish*ed*
furni/ture
furore
fur/*rier*
fur/row*ed*
further/*ance*
fur/thest
furt/ive*ly*
fus*ed*
fusel/age
fusib/il/ity
fusil/ier
fusil/lade
fu/sion
fus/tian
futil/ity
futur/ism
futur/ity
fuzzy

G

gabar/dine
gabl*ed*
gadget
gaffer
gage ↔ gauge
gaiety
gaily
gait
gala
gal/axy
gal/lan*try*

gall*ed*
gal/leon
galler/ies
galleys
Gallic
galli/vant/*ing*
gallon/*age*
gal/lop*ed* ↔
    galop*ed*
gallo/way (G)
galop ↔ gallop
galore
ga/loshes *also*
    go/loshes
galvan/iz*ed*
gambit
gambl*ed*
gam/boge
gambol*led*
gamete
gamma
gammon*ed*
gamut
gamy
gan/glion
gan/gren*ed*
gangren/ous
gannet
gantry
gaol*er also* jail*er*
garag*ed*
garb/age
garb*ed*
garbl*ed*
garçon
gar/denia
gargan/tuan

gargl*ed*
gar/goyle
garish*ly*
gar/land*ed*
gar/lic*ky*
garnet
gar/nish*ed*
garret
gar/rison*ed*
gar/rott*ed also*
    gar/ott*ed*
garru/lity
garrul/ous*ly*
gas/*eous*
gas*es*
gas*ol/ine*
gaso/meter
gass*ed*
gassy
gastro/nomic
gastro/pod
gât/eau
gate/way
gaucher*ie*
gau/chos
gaudy
gauge ↔ gage
gauge/*able*
gauging
gaunt/let
gauze
gauzy
gavel
ga/votte
gawky
gaz/elle
gazett/e*er*

gecko(*e*)s
geisha
gelat/ine
gelatin/ous
geld/*ing*
gelig/nite
gel*led*
gendarm/*erie*
gender
genea/logical
genera **p**
general/*ization*
gener/ator
generic/*ally*
gener/os/ity
gener/ous*ly*
gen/*csis*
gen/*etic*
genetic/*ally*
geni/al/*ity*
genie [genii]
gen/ital
genit/ive
geni/us*es or*
    genii
geno/cide
genre
gen/teel*ly*
gen/tian
gen/tile
gentil/ity
gently
genu/flexion
genu/ine
genus [genera]
geo/centric
geo/desy

geo/graphic/al*ly*

geo/logy

geo/metric/al*ly*

geo/metry

geo/morphology

geor/gette

Geor/gian

gera/nium

geri/atric*s*

ger/mane

Ger/man*ic*

german/ium

germi/*cidal*

germin/ate*d*

geronto/logy

gerry/mandere*d*

gerund/*ive*

ges/talt (G)

gesta/tion

gesticu/late*d*

ges/ture*d*

get/*table*

gew/gaw

geyser

ghastli/ness

ghastly

gher/kin

ghetto*s*

ghost*ly*

ghoul/*ishly*

giant

gibber/*ish*

gibbet

gibbon

gib/bous

gibe

gib/lets

gigantic/*ally*

gig/olo*s*

gild ↔ guild

gild*ed*

gills

gilt

gim/mick

ginger

ging/ham

gingiv/itis

gin/seng

gipsy *use* gypsy

gir/affe

girder

girdl*ed*

girth

gist

giz/zard

gla/cial

gla/cier

gladi/ator/*ial*

gladi/olus*es* (oli)

glamor/ous*ly*

glam/our

gland*u*/lar

glare*d*

glauc/oma

glaze*d*

glaz/ier

gleaner

glebe

glee/ful*ly*

glimpse*d*

gliss/ade

glis/tene*d*

gloam/ing

gloat/ing*ly*

global

globe

globu/lar

glocken/spiel

glori/fy*ing*

glori/ous*ly*

gloss/*ary*

glot/tis

gluc/ose

gluing

gluten

glutin/ous

glutton/ous*ly*

glycer/ine

gnarle*d*

gnashe*d*

gnat

gnawe*d*

gnome

gnomic

gnos/tic

gnu

goade*d*

goanna

goatee

Gob/elin

goblet

goblin

god/*dess*

goffer

goitre

goit/rous

golli/wog

go/loshes *also*

   ga/loshes

gonad

gon/dolas

gondo/lier

gonor/rhoea

good/bye

googly

goose/berry

gopher

gore*d*

gorge

gor/geous*ly*

gorgo/n*ian*

gor/illa

gormand/ize*d*

gorse

gos/ling

gospel/*ler*

gos/samer

gos/sipe*d*

gouged

gou/lash

gourd

gour/mand

gour/met

govern/*ance*

govern/*mental*

gov/erno*r*

gra/cious*ly*

grad/ate*d*

grada/tion

gradi/ent

gradu/al*ly*

gradu/and

gradu/ate

graf/fito [fiti]

grail (G)

gram

gramin/aceous

gramini/vorous

grammar/*ian*
grammatic/al*ly*
gramo/phone
grana/dilla
gran/ary
grand/*eur*
grandi/loquent
grandi/ose*ly*
gran/ite
grani/vorous
grano/lith*ic*
grant*ee*
granu/lar
granu/lat*ed*
graphic/*ally*
graph/ite
grap/nel
grappl*ed*
grat*ed*
grate/ful*ly*
grati/fy*ing*
gratin
gratis
gratit/ude
gratu/itous*ly*
grav/el*ly*
gravit/at*ed*
gravita/tion*al*
grav/ity
gravy
gra/zier
grease **n/v**
greasy
great*ly*
Grecian
Greece
Greek

green/*ness*
greet/*ings*
gregari/ous*ly*
gren/ade
grena/dier
grena/dilla *use*
  grana/dilla
grenad/ine
griddl*ed*
grief
griev/ance
grieve
griev/ous*ly*
grif/fin
grill **n/v**
grille *also* grill
grim/ac*ed*
grimy
grip*ed*
grip*ped*
grisly
gristly
grizzl*ed*
grizzly
grocery
grog*gy*
groin
grom/met
groovy
grop*ed*
gross*ly*
grot/esque*ly*
grot/to/(*e*)s
grouch*ed*
ground/sel
group*ed*
grous*ed*

grovell*ed*
grow*th*
groyne
grudging*ly*
gruel
grue/some*ly*
Gruy/ère
gryphon *use*
  griffin
gua/nos
guaran/teed
guar/antor
guard/*ian*
guava
guer/illa *also*
  guer/rilla
guess*ed*
guest
guf/faw*ed*
guid/ance
guid*ed*
guild ↔ gild
guilder
guile/ful*ly*
guillot/ine*d*
guilty
Guinea
guise
guitar/*ist*
gules
gullet
gully
gump/tion
gun/*nery*
gunny
gun/whale
gurgita/tion

gurgl*ed*
Gurkha
gurn/ard
guru
gus/set*ed*
gustat/ory
gusto
gutta-/percha
gut/tural
gybe
gym/khana
gymnas/ium
gym/nast*ic*
gypsum
gypsy
gyrat*ed*
gyro/scope

H

hab/eas cor/pus
haber/dashery
habili/ment
habit/*able*
hab/it*at*
habitu/al*ly*
hack/neys
Hades
haemat/ite
haemo/globin
haemo/phil/*iac*
haemor/rhage
haemor/roids
hag/gard
haggis
haggl*ed*

hagi/ology

hail

hal/cyon

hale

halit/osis [ses]

hallelujah *also*
   alleluia

halliard *use*
   halyard

hallo *also* hello,
   hullo

hallo*oed*

hallow*ed*

hallucin/atory

halo*es*

halv*ed*

hal/yard

ham/burger (H)

hamlet

hammer*ed*

ham/mock

hand/ful*s*

handi/cap*per*

handi/craft

hand/kerchief*s*

hand/some*ly*

hangar

hang*er*

hansom cab

hap/hazard*ly*

happen*ed*

happi/ness

hara-/kiri

har/angu*ed*

harass*ed*

harbin/ger

harbour/*age*

hardi/hood

harem

hari/cot

harlequin/*ade*

harmon/ica

harmon/ies

harmoni/ous*ly*

har/ness*ed*

har/poon*ed*

harpsi/chord

harque/bus*es*

har/ridan

har/rier

hart

harte/beest

har/vest*er*

hash/ish

has/sock

hasten*ed*

hastily

hasty

hatch/*ery*

hatchet

hatred

haughty

haul/*age*

haul/*ier*

haunch

haunt*ed*

haver/sack

hav/ing

havoc

hawser

haw/thorn

hazard/*ous*

hazy

head/ache

health/*ily*

hearken*ed*

hearse

hearth*s*

heart/*ily*

heathen/*ness*

heather

heath*s*

heav/en*ly*

Heb/raic

Hebrew

heca/tomb

hectic/*ally*

hedon/ism

hege/mony

heifer

heighten*ed*

hein/ous*ly*

heir/loom

heli/copter

helio/tropic

helium

helle/bore

Hellen/ism

hello *also* hallo,
   hullo

helm*ed*

hel/met*ed*

helot

hen/deca/gon

hen/diadys

hepat/itis

hepta/gon*al*

hepta/meter

her/ald*ry*

herb/*aceous*

herb/*age*

herbal/*ist*

herb/*ar/ium*

heredit/ary

heresy [ies]

her/et/ic/al*ly*

herit/able

herm/aphrod/ite

hermetic/*ally*

hermit/*age*

her/nial

hero*es* **m**

heroic/*ally*

heroin

hero/ine*s* **f**

heron

herpeto/logy

her/ring-bone

hesit/ant*ly*

hesita/tion

hes/sian

hetero/dox

hetero/dyne

hetero/gen/eous

heur/istic

hewer

hexa/gon*al*

hexa/meter

hey/day

hiatus*es*

hibern/at*ed*

hibis/cus*es*

hic/cup*ed also*
   hic/cough*ed*

hick/ory

hid*den*

hid/eous*ly*

hie

hier/archy

hiero/glyph*ic*

hiero/phant*ic*

hi-fi

high*ly*

hijack

hilari/ous*ly*

hilar/ity

hil/*lock*

hinder*ed*

Hindi

hind/rance

Hindu/*ism*

Hindu/stani

hinge*ing*

hinter/land

hippo/
   potamus*es*

hire/*ling*

hir/sute

histor/ian

historic/al*ly*

histri/onic

hither

hoard*ed*

hoard/*ing*

hoarse*ly*

hoary

hoax*er*

hobby/*ist*

hob/goblin

hob-/nobb*ed*

hobo(*e*)s

hockey

hocus-/pocus

hodo/meter *use*
   odo/meter

hoe/*ing*

hogget

hog/manay

hoi polloi

hoist*ed*

hokey-/pokey

holi/day*ed*

holily

holi/ness

holism

holly/hock

holo/caust

hol/ster

holus-/bolus

holy

hom/age

home/*stead*

hom/icidal

homily

hominy

homoe/opathy

homo/gen/eity

homo/geneous*ly*

homogen/iz*ed*

homo/logue

hom/onym

homo/phone

homo/sexual

homun/cule

hon*ed*

hon/esty

honey/comb*ed*

honor/ariums
   [*or* ria]

honor/ary

honour/*able*

hood/lum

hoo/doos

hoofs *also*
   hooves

hookah

hooligan/*ism*

hoop-la

hope/ful*ly*

hoping

hop/*ping*

horary

horde

hori/zon*tal*

hor/mone

hornet

horny

horo/logist

horo/scope

hor/rible

horrid

horri/fy/*ing*

horror

hors d'oeuvre

horsy

hort/atory

horti/cultural

hos/anna

hosi/ery

hos/pice

hospit/able

hos/pit/ality

host/*age*

hos/tel*ry*

hostil/ity

hotel/*ier*

house/wife*ry*

hovel

hover/craft

how/dah

how/itzer

hoyden/*ish*

hubbub

hub/rist*ic*

hucka/back

huddl*ed*

hu*ed*

huge*ly*

hula

hulla/baloo

hullo *also* hello,
   hallo

human

humane

human/itar/ian

human/*ness*

humbly

hu/merus

humid/*ity*

humili/at*ed*

humil/ity

hum/mock

humor/ist

humor/ous*ly*

humus

hun/dred*th*

Hun/*nish*

hurd/ler

hurdy-/gurdy

hurl*ed*

hurly-/burly

hur/rah*ed*

hurric/ane

hur/ried*ly*

hurry/*ing*

hurtl*ed*

hus/band*ry*
husky
hussar
hussy
hustle*d*
hy/acinth
hyal/ine
hybrid/*ism*
hy/datid
hydra
hydran/gea
hy/drant
hy/drated
hy/draulic
hydro/chloric
hydro/electric
hydrogen/ated
hydro/pathy
hydro/phobia
hydro/ponics
hydrox/ide
hy/droxyl
hy/ena
hy/giene
hygienic/*ally*
hymen
hymn*al*
hym/n*ody*
hyoid
hyper/aesthesia
hyper/bola
hyper/bole
hyper/bolic
hyper/borean
hyper/critical
hyper/metrical
hyper/tension

hyphen
hyphen/ated
hypno/sis
hypnotic/*ally*
hypo/chondriac
hypo/crisy
hypo/critical
hypo/dermic/
    ally
hypoten/use
hypo/thesis
hypo/thes/ized
hypo/thetic*al*
hyssop
hyster/ectomy
hys/teria
hyster/ical

I

iambic
lber/ian
ibex*es*
ibis*es*
ice/berg
Ice/land*ic*
icicle
icing
iconic *also*
    ikon*ic*
icono/clast*ic*
icono/logy
icy
idea
ideal/istic/*ally*
ideal*ly*

identic/al*ly*
identi/fica/tion
iden/tity
ideo/logic/al*ly*
idi/ocy
idio/matic/*ally*
idio/syncrasy
idio/syncratic
idiotic/*ally*
idle
idly
idol/*atrous*
idyllic/*ally*
igloo
igne/ous
ignite*d*
igni/tion
ig/noble
ignomini/ous*ly*
igno/miny
ignor/amus*es*
ignor/ance
iguana
ikonic *also*
    iconic
iliac
iliad (I)
illegal/*ity*
il/legible
illegit/imate
illiber/al/*ity*
il/licit*ly*
illimit/able
illiter/acy
illiter/ate
illogic/al*ity*
illumin/ated

illusion/*ist*
illus/ory
illus/trat/ive
illus/tri/ous
imagery
imagin/able
imagin/ary
imaginat/ive*ly*
im/becile
imbed*ded* also
    em/bedded
imbibe*d*
imbro/glios
imbue*d*
imit/ative*ly*
immacu/late*ly*
im/manent
immateri/al/*ity*
im/mature*ly*
immeasur/ably
immedi/acy
immedi/ate*ly*
immemori/al*ly*
immense*ly*
im/mersed
immig/rate
immin/ent
immob/ility
immoder/ate*ly*
im/modesty
immol/ated
immoral/*ity*
immortal/*ity*
immov/able
immun/ized
immured
immut/able

impacted

impala

impale/*ment*

impalp/ably

im/panel*led also*
   em/panel*led*

imparti/al*ity*

impass/able

im/passe

impass/ible

impass/ive*ly*

im/patient*ly*

impeach/*ment*

impec/cable

impecuni/ous*ly*

imped/ance

impede*d*

impedi/ment

im/pel*led*

impend

impenet/rable

impenit/ence

imperat/ive*ly*

impercept/ible

im/perfection

imperi/al/*ism*

im/peril*led*

imperi/ous*ly*

imperish/able

imperman/ent

im/per/meable

imperson/al*ly*

impertin/ent*ly*

imperturb/ably

impervi/ous*ly*

im/petigo

impetu/osity

impetu/ous*ly*

im/petus

im/piety

impinge/*ment*

im/pious

implac/able

implaus/ible

imple/mented

implic/ated

implica/tion

impli/cit*ly*

im/plored

imply/*ing*

im/polite*ly*

imponder/able

import/*able*

import/*ance*

importun/ate*ly*

imposi/tion

imposs/ibil/ity

imposs/ible

impostor

impost/ure

impot/ent*ly*

impractic/able

impreca/tion

impreg/nable

impreg/nated

impres/arios

impression/*able*

impression/*ism*

im/prisoned

imprison/*ment*

improb/able

im/promptu*s*

impropri/ety

improv/abil/ity

improvid/ent*ly*

impro/visa/tion

impud/ence

impugn/*ment*

impuls/ive*ly*

impun/ity

impur/ity

imput/able

impute

inabil/ity

in/access/ible

in/accur/acy

in/accur/ate

in/adequacy

in/adequate*ly*

in/admiss/ible

in/advert/ent*ly*

in/advis/able

in/alien/able

inane

in/anim/ate

inani/tion

in/appeas/able

in/appell/able

in/applic/able

in/appos/ite

in/appreciable

in/apprehens/
   ible

in/approach/
   able

in/appropri/ate

in/articu/late

in/artist/ic/*ally*

in/atten/tion

in/audible

inaug/ur/al*ly*

in/auspici/ous*ly*

in/calcul/able

incandes/ce*nt*

in/capable

in/capacit/ated

in/capacity

incarcer/ator

in/carna/dined

incarna/tion

in/cautious*ly*

incendi/ary

in/censed

incent/ive

incep/tion

in/certi/tude

incess/ant*ly*

incestu/ous*ly*

incho/ate

incid/ence

incident/al*ly*

inciner/ator

incipi/ent

incised

in/cision

incisor

incited

in/clem/ent

inclina/tion

inclus/ive*ly*

incog/nito

in/cogniz/able

in/coher/ence

in/cohes/ive

in/combust/ible

in/commensur/
   able

in/com/moded

in/commodi/ous
in/communic/
    able
in/communic/
    ado
in/communicat/
    ive
in/compar/able
in/compatible
in/compet/ency
in/complete*ly*
in/compre/hens/
    ible
in/compress/ible
in/conceiv/able
in/conclus/ive
in/condens/able
in/congru/ity
in/congru/ous*ly*
in/consequen/
    tial
in/consider/able
in/consider/ate
in/consist/ency
in/consist/ent
in/consol/able
in/conspicu/ous
in/constancy
in/contest/able
in/contro/vert/
    ible
in/conveni/
    enc*ed*
in/convert/ible
inco/ordina/tion
incorpor/at*ed*
in/corpor/eal

in/cor/rigible
in/corrupt/ible
in/creas*ed*
in/cred/ible
in/credu/lous*ly*
in/crement
incrimin/atory
incub/ator
in/cubus
incul/cat*ed*
incum/bent
in/curably
in/curi/ous
in/cur*red*
incur/sion
in/debted
in/decent*ly*
in/decipher/able
in/decis/ive*ly*
in/decor/ous*ly*
in/decorum
in/defatig/able
in/defeas/ible
in/defens/ible
in/defin/able
in/defin/ite*ly*
in/delible
in/delic/ate*ly*
indemni/fy*ing*
indenta/*tion*
inden/tur*ed*
independ/ence
in/describ/able
in/destruct/ible
in/determin/able
in/determin/ate
in/determin/ism

index*es also*
    indices
indicat/ive*ly*
indic/ator
in/dices *also*
    index*es*
indict/*able*
in/differ/ence
indigen/ous
in/digest/ible
indig/nant*ly*
in/dignity
indigo*s*
in/direct*ly*
in/discern/ible
in/discerpt/ible
in/discip/line
in/discreet
in/discrete
in/discre/tion
in/discrimin/ate
in/dispens/able
indisposi/tion
in/disput/able
in/dissol/uble
in/distinct*ly*
in/distin/guish/
    able
indit*ed*
indi/vidual/*ity*
in/divis/ible
indoctrin/at*ed*
indol/ent*ly*
in/domit/able
in/dubit/able
induce/*ment*
in/duction

in/duc*tor*
indul/ge*nce*
induna
indus/trial/*ist*
industri/ous*ly*
inebri/at*ed*
inebri/ety
in/edible
in/effable
in/efface/able
in/effectu/al*ly*
in/effica/cious*ly*
in/effic/iency
in/effi/ciently
in/eleg/ant*ly*
in/eligible
in/eluct/able
in/ept*it*/*ude*
in/equable
in/equal/ity
in/equit/able
in/equity
in/eradic/able
iner/*tia*
in/escap/able
in/essen/tial
in/estim/able
in/evit/able
in/excus/able
in/exhaust/ible
in/exor/able
in/expedi/ent
in/expens/ive*ly*
in/expi/able
in/explic/able
in/expli/cit
in/express/ible

in/extinguish/
   able
in/extric/able
in/fallibil/ism
in/fallible
in/famous*ly*
infamy
in/fancy
in/fanta
infanti/*cide*
infant/*ile*
infan/try
infatu/ation
in/fect*ious*
in/felicit/ous
infer/*able*
infer/*ence*
infer/ential*ly*
inferi/or*ity*
infern/al*ly*
infer/*nos*
infer*red*
in/fertil/ity
infesta/*tion*
infidel/*ity*
infilt/rat*ed*
infin/ite*ly*
infinit/esim/
   al*ly*
infinit/ive
infin/ity
infirm/*ary*
in/flam*ed*
inflam/mable
inflamma/tion
inflammat/ory
inflation/*ary*

inflex/ion *also*
   inflect/ion
influ/ence
influ/ential
influ/enza
in/fold*ed also*
   en/fold*ed*
infra-/red
in/frequency
infringe/*ment*
infuri/at*ed*
ingeni/ous*ly*
ingénue
ingenu/ity
ingenu/ous*ly*
inges/*tion*
ingle-nook
ingrati/ating
in/gratit/ude
ingredi/ent
in/gress
in/gurgita/tion
inhabit/*ant*
in/hal*ed*
in/harmoni/ous
in/herent*ly*
inherit/*ance*
inhibi/*tion*
inhibit/*ory*
in/homo/
   geneous
in/hospit/able
in/human
in/humane
inim/ical
in/imit/able
iniquit/ous

ini/quity
ini/tial*led*
initi/ation
initi/ative
initi/ator
in/judi/cious*ly*
in/junction
injuri/ous*ly*
injury
ink/ling
in/nate*ly*
in/navig/able
in/nings
inno/cence
innocu/ous*ly*
innova/tion
innu/endo*es*
in/numer/able
in/numer/ate
inocu/lat*ed*
in/offens/ive*ly*
in/oper/able
in/oppor/tune*ly*
in/ordin/ate*ly*
in/organic
input
in/quest
in/quiet/ude
in/quire *also*
   enquire
inquisit/ive*ly*
inquisit/or/*ial*
in/sanit/ary
in/sati/able
inscrip/tion
in/scrut/able
insect/*icidal*

insect/*ivore*
insemin/at*ed*
in/sens/ate*ly*
in/sens/ibil/ity
in/sentient
in/separ/able
in/sert*ion*
insidi/ous*ly*
insig/nia
in/signi/fic/ant
in/sincere*ly*
insinu/at*ed*
in/sipid/*ity*
insist/*ence*
insist/*ent*
in/sobri/ety
insol/ence
insol/uble
in/solv/ency
insom/nia
inspector/*ate*
inspira/tion
in/stabil/ity
installa/*tion*
instal/ment
instant/*aneous*
instig/ator
in/stil
in/stilled
instinc/tive*ly*
insti/tut*ed*
institu/tion
in/struct*or*
instru/ment*al*
in/subordin/ate
in/substan/tial
in/suffer/able

in/suffi/ciency
insular/ity
insu/lation
insu/lin
insulted
in/super/able
in/support/
    able
insur/ance
insured
insur/gent
in/surmount/
    able
insur/rection
in/suscept/ible
in/taglios
in/tan/gible
in/teger
integ/ral
integ/rated
integ/rity
integu/ment
intel/lectual
intelli/gence
intelli/gentsia
intelli/gibil/ity
in/temper/ately
in/tense/ly
intens/ity
intention/ally
inter/active
inter/ceded
inter/ception
inter/cession
inter/
    communica/
    tion

inter/
    communion
inter/
    connect/ing
inter/depend/
    ence
inter/dict/ion
inter/estedly
inter/ference
inter/fused
in/terim
inter/ior
inter/jectory
inter/linear
inter/locutor
inter/loper
inter/lude
inter/mediary
inter/medi/ate
inter/ment
in/termin/ably
inter/mission
inter/mittently
inter/national
inter/necine
intern/ed
inter/pellate
inter/penetrated
inter/polator
inter/posed
interpreta/tions
inter/preted
in/terr/ed
inter/regnum
inter/rela/tion
interrog/ation
interrogat/ive

interrog/atory
inter/rupter
inter/section
inter/spersed
inter/stice
inter/val
inter/vened
inter/vention
inter/view
in/test/ate
intest/ine
intim/acy
intim/ated
intimid/atory
in/toler/able
in/toler/antly
intona/tion
intoxic/ant
intoxic/ate
in/tract/able
in/trans/igent
in/trepid
intric/acy
in/trigued
intrinsic/ally
intro/duced
intro/ductory
intro/spect/ively
intro/verted
in/truder
intru/sion
intuit/ively
inund/ated
inured
in/utility
invaded
in/valid/ated

in/valu/ably
in/vari/ably
inva/sion
invect/ive
in/veigh/ed
inveigle/ment
in/ventor
invent/ory
in/verse/ly
in/version
in/verteb/rate
investig/atory
investit/ure
inveter/ate
invidi/ously
invigor/ated
invin/cible
in/viol/able
in/visib/il/ity
invita/tion
invoca/tion
invoc/atory
in/voice
invoked
in/volun/tar/ily
involu/tion
involve/ment
in/vulner/able
iodine
ion
Ionic
ion/ium
iono/sphere
iota
ipecacu/anha
Iraqi
iras/cible

irate*ly*
irides/cent
iri/dium
iris*es*
Irish/*ism*
irk/*some*
iron*ed*
ironic/al*ly*
irony
irradi/ation
irration/al*ity*
ir/reclaim/able
ir/reconcil/able
ir/redeem/able
ir/redu/cible
ir/refrag/able
ir/refut/able
ir/regu/lar*ity*
ir/relev/ance
ir/relev/ant*ly*
ir/remedi/able
ir/remov/able
ir/repar/able
ir/replace/able
ir/repress/ible
ir/reproach/able
ir/resist/ible
ir/resol/ute*ly*
ir/respect/ive
ir/respon/sible
ir/retriev/able
ir/rever/ent*ly*
ir/revers/ible
ir/revoc/able
irrig/ate*d*
irrit/able
irrit/ant

ir/rupt*ion*
ls/lam*ic*
island
islet
iso/bar
iso/hyet
isol/ate*d*
iso/metric
iso/sceles
iso/therm
iso/tope
lsrael/*ite*
issue*d*
issu/ing
isth/mus
ltali/an/*ate*
ital/iciz*ed*
item/iz*ed*
itiner/ant
itiner/ary
ivory

J

jab/ber*ed*
jaca/randa
jackal
jackass
jag/uar
jail*er also*
    gaol*er*
jalap
ja/lopy
Ja/maic*an*
jamb
jamboree

janiss/ary *also*
    janiz/ary
jan/itor
Janu/ary
Japan/*ese*
ja/pan*ned*
japon/ica
jargon
jarrah
jas/mine
jasper
jaun/dic*ed*
jaunty
Javan/*ese*
jav/elin
jeal/ous*y*
Jeho/vah
jejune
jeopard/ize
jeop/ardy
Jere/miah
jersey (J)
Jeru/salem
jester
Jesuit/ic/al*ly*
jetsam
jet/tison*ed*
jetty
jew/ell*ed*
jewel/*ler*
jewel/*lery*
Jewry
jib*bed*
jibe *use* gibe
jingo/*ism*
jockey*ed*
jockey*s*

joc/ose*ly*
jocu/lar/*ity*
jocund/*ity*
jodh/purs
joie de vivre
joist*ed*
jol/lity
Jonah
jon/quil
jostl*ed*
journal/*ist*
jour/ney*ed*
jour/neys
joust*ed*
jovi/al*ity*
Jovian
jubi/lant
jubila/tion
jubilee
Ju/daic
judder*ed*
judge
judge/ment *also*
    judg/ment
judic/ature
judici/al*ly*
judi/ciary
judi/cious*ly*
jugger/naut
jug/gler
Jugo/slav*ia use*
    Yugoslav*ia*
jug/ular
juicy
ju-jitsu
ju/jube
julep

junction

junc/ture

jungly

juni/per

junket/*ing*

junta

Ju/piter

jurid/ical

juris/diction

juris/prudence

juror

just/ice

justici/ary

justifi/able

justi/fies

juven/ile

juven/ilia

K

kaiser

kaleido/scope

kangaroo

kaolin

kapok

karate

karma

kauri

kava

kayak

kedge

kedgeree

keen/*ness*

kelpie

kennel*led*

ker/atin

kerb ↔ curb **n**

ker/chief

kernel

keros/ene *also*
    keros/ine

kes/trel

ketch

ketone

key*ed*

khaki

khan

kib/butz*im*

kidnap/*per*

kidney*s*

kiln

kilo/gram

kilo/metre

kimo/no*s*

kinder/garten

kindle*d*

kind/red

kin/etic

kiosk

kip/per*ed*

kirk

kismet

kitchen/*ette*

kitten/*ish*

klaxon

klepto/maniac

kloof

knacker

knap/sack

knavish*ly*

knead*ed*

kneel*ed*

knell*ed*

knicker/bocker

knick/knack

knight*ly*

knit/*ting*

knob*bly*

knoll

knot*ty*

know/*ledge*

know/ledge/*able*

knuckle

koala*s*

kohl/rabi

ko/peck *also* ko/
    pec, co/peck

Koran

kosher

kowtow

kraal

krait

kraken

krem/lin

krone

krypton

Kurd

L

laa/ger ↔ la/ger

label*led*

labial

laborat/ory

labori/ous*ly*

labour*ed*

laburnum

laby/rinth/*ine*

lacer/ate*d*

lachrym/atory

lachrym/ose

lacka/daisical

lackeys *also*
    lacqueys

laconic/*ally*

lacquer*ed*

lacqueys *also*
    lackeys

lacta/tion

lacteal

lact/ose

lacun/ary

lacy

lad/dered

ladies

ladle*d*

lady/*ship*

lager ↔ laa/ger

lagoon

lair

laissez-/*faire*

laity

lam/baste*d*

lamb/*kin*

lamel/late*d*

lament/*able*

lamin/ate*d*

laming/ton

lam/poon*ed*

lam/preys

lance*t*

lan/guage

lan/guidly

lan/guished

languor/ous*ly*

lan/olin

lan/tern
lan/yard
lapel
lapid/ary
lapis lazuli
Lap/land*er*
Lapp
lapsed
lar/ceny
lar/gess *also* lar/
   gesse
largo
lariat
larri/kin
larva*e*
laryn/geal
laryn/gitis
larynx
lascivi/ous*ly*
lassi/tude
lasso*s*
latent
late*r*
lat/eral*ly*
latex
lath
lathe
lather*ed*
Latin/*ate*
latit/ude
lat/rine
latter
lat/tice*d*
Lat/via*n*
laud/*able*
laud/anum
laud/*atory*

laugh/*able*
laugh/*ter*
launch*ed*
laun/der*ed*
launder/*ette*
laund/ress
laundro/mat
laundry
laure/ate
laurel*led*
lava
lav/atory
laven/der
law*yer*
lax*at/ive*
layer*ed*
lay/ette
lazi/ness
lea
leach*ed*
lead
lead*en*
leaf/*let*
league
leak ↔ leek
lean/*ness*
learn*ed*
lease/hold*er*
least
leather/*ette*
leaven*ed*
lecher/ous*ly*
lec/tern
lec/ture*r*
led
ledger
leech

leek ↔ leak
leery
lee/*ward*
leg/acy
legal/*ity*
leg/ate
lega/tion
legend/*ary*
legible
legion/*ary*
legis/lator
legis/lature
legitim/ate*ly*
legitim/ize*d*
legume
legumin/ous
lei*s*
leis/ure*ly*
lem/ming
lemon/*ade*
lemur
length*y*
leni/ency
lenity
lens*es*
lentil
leon/ine
leo/pard
leo/tard
leper
lepid/opter/ous
lep/rechaun
lep/rosy
lep/rous
les/bian (L)
lesion
lessee

lessen*ed*
lesson
lessor
lethal
leth/argy
letter/*ing*
let/tuce
leuco/tomy
leuk/aemia
levee
level*led*
lever*ed*
lev/eret
levi/athan
levit/ate*d*
Levit/icus
lev/ity
levy/*ing*
lewd
lexico/grapher
lex/icon
liabil/ity
liable
li/aise
li/aison
liana
liar
libel/*lous*
liber/ali*ty*
libera/tion
liber/tar/ian
lib/erty
libidin/ous
libido
libra
librar/ian
lib/rary

lib/retto [tti *or*
  ttos]
Libya*n*
li/cence **n**
li/censed **v**
licens*ee*
licenti/ate
licenti/ous*ly*
lichen
licit*ly*
licorice *also*
  liquor/ice
lied*er*
lief
liege
lien
lieu
lieuten/ant
liga/ment
ligat/ure
lighten/*ing*
light/*ning*
lig/neous
lig/nite
like/*able*
likeli/hood
lilac
li-lo
lily [ies]
limb
limbo*s*
limer/ick
lim/it*ed*
limous/ine
limpid
linage
linden

lineage
lin/eal
linea/ment*s*
linear
linen
lin/gerie
lingua franca
lin/gual
lin/guist*ic*
lini/ment
linnet
lino/leum
lino/type
lin/seed
lintel
lion/iz*ed*
lique/fy/*ing*
liques/cent
li/queur
liquid*a*/tion
liquid/*ity*
liquor
liquor/ice *also*
  licorice
lisle
lissom *also*
  lissome
lis/ten*er*
list/less*ly*
litany
liter/acy
liter/al*ly*
liter/ary
liter/ature
lithe/*some*
litho/graph*ic*
litho/graph*y*

Lithu/an/ia*n*
litiga/tion
litigi/ous
litmus
li/totes
litre
litter*ed*
lit/toral
litur/gical
live
liv/able *also*
  live/able
liveli/hood
liveli/ness
liv/ery
liv/id*ity*
lizard
llama
load*ed*
loaf [loaves]
loamy
loath **a**
loathe **v**
loath/some
lobby/*ist*
lob/*ectomy*
local **a**
locale **n**
loch
loco/motive
loco/motory
locum tenens
locus [loci]
lode
lodge
lodging
lodge/ment

logan/berry
log/arithm*ic*
logger/heads
loggia*s*
logic/al*ity*
logist/ics
logo*s*
loin*s*
loi/ter*er*
loll*ed*
loneli/*ness*
longev/ity
longit/udinal
loofah
loose*ly*
loosen*ed*
loqua/cious*ly*
loquat
lore
lorg/nette
loris
lory
lose
losing
loth **a**
Lo/thario
lotion
lot/tery
lotto
lotus
loung*er*
louse
lousy
louvre
Louvre
lovable
loveli/*ness*

loy/al*ty*
loz/enge
lubber
lubric/ant
lubric/ate*d*
lucent
lu/cern *also* lu/
 cerne
lucid/*ity*
Luci/fer
lucrat/ive*ly*
lucre
lucub/rate*d*
ludic/rous*ly*
lug/gage
lugubri/ous*ly*
luke/warm
lul/*laby*
lum/bago
lum/bar
lum/ber
lumin/ary
lumin/osity
lumin/ous*ly*
lun/acy
lunar
lun/atic
lunch/*eon*
lun/ette
lunge*d*
lupin *also* lupine
lup/ine
lurch*er*
lure*d*
lurid*ly*
lurk
lus/cious*ly*

lush*ly*
lustre
lus/trous*ly*
lutan/ist *also*
 luten/ist
lute
Luth/era*n*
luxuri/ant*ly*
luxuri/ous*ly*
lux/ury
lyc/anthropy
lychee *use* litchi
lye
lying
lymph/*atic*
lynch*ed*
lynx-/*eyed*
lyre-/*bird*
lyric/al*ly*
Lysol

M

ma/cabre
macadam/ize*d*
macar/oni
macar/oon
Macas/sar
macaw
mace
macer/ate*d*
Mach
ma/chete
Machi/avel/li*an*
machin/ator
ma/chiner*y*

ma/chinist
mack/erel
mack/intosh
mac/ramé
macro/cosmi*c*
macron
macu/la*e*
macu/la*r*
madam
Madame
madden/ing*ly*
Ma/deira
ma/donna
mad/rigal
mael/strom
maenad
maes/tro
mafia (M)
maga/zine
magenta
mag/got*y*
magi/cia*n*
magisteri/al*ly*
magis/trate
magis/trat/ure
magma
Magna Charta
magnan/imity
magnanim/ous*ly*
mag/nate
mag/nesia
magnet/ic/al*ly*
magnet/iz/*ing*
magneto/*motive*
mag/neto*s*
magni/ficat
magni/ficence

magni/fico*es*
magni/fy*ing*
magni/loquent*ly*
magni/tude
mag/nolia*s*
Magyar
maha/raja *also*
 maha/rajah
Ma/hatma
mah-jong *also*
 mah-jongg
mahog/any
maid/en*ly*
mai/eutic
maim*ed*
maintain/*able*
mainten/ance
maître d'hôtel
maize
majest/ic*ally*
major/*ity*
malach/ite
mal/adjust/*ment*
mal/adroit
malady
mal/aise
malaprop/*ism*
mal/aria
Malay/sia*n*
mal/ediction
mal/efactor
mal/eficent*ly*
mal/evolent*ly*
mal/feasance
mali/cious*ly*
malig/nant*ly*
malig/ni*ty*

malin/ger*er*
mal/lard
mal/leable
mallet
malmsey
mal/nutrition
mal/odor/ous*ly*
mal/practice
mal/versa/tion
mamil/la*ry*
mamma/*lian*
mammon/*ite*
mam/moths
man/acl*ed*
manage/*able*
manage/*ment*
manager/ial*ly*
man/darin
mandatory
mand/ible
man/dolin *also*
  man/doline
man/drel
man/drill
man/euvre*d* *use*
  manoeuvre*d*
mangan/ese
mange
manger
man/*goes*
mangy
mania*c*
manic
Mani/chaean
mani/cure*d*
manicur/ist
mani/festo*s*

mani/fold
man/*ikin* ↔
  man/nequin
manila (M)
ma/nilla
manioc
manip/ulator
manna
man/nequin ↔
  man/*ikin*
manner*ed*
manner/*ism*
man/*nish*
man/oeuvre*d*
man/or*ial*
manqué
manse
man/sion
mantel/piece
man/tilla
mantis
man/tissa*e*
mantle
manu/al*ly*
manu/facturer
manure*d*
manu/script
Manx
Maori*s*
maple
maras/chino*s*
ma/raude*r*
marbly
marcas/ite
marchion/ess
mare
margar/ine

margin/al*ly*
marguer/ite
mari/gold
mari/huana *also*
  mari/juana
ma/rimba
marin/ade **n**
marin/ate **v**
mar/ine*r*
mari/onette
mar/ital
mari/time
mar/joram
mar/kete*d*
marma/lade
marmo/set
maroone*d*
mar/quee
mar/quess
mar/quis **m**
mar/quise **f**
marr*ed*
marriage/*able*
marrow
Marseil/laise
mar/shalle*d*
marsup/ial
marten
mar/tial
Mar/tian
martin
mar/tinet
martin/gale
mar/tini
martyr/*dom*
mar/velle*d*
marvel/lous*ly*

Marx/*ian*
marzi/pan
mas/cara
mascot
mascu/line
mascu/lin/ity
masoch/ism
ma/son*ry*
masquer/ade*d*
mas/sacre*d*
mas/sage*d*
mas/se*s*
mas/seur **m**
mas/seuse **f**
massif
mas/sive*ly*
master/piece
mastic/ate*d*
mas/tiff
mast/itis
masto/don
masturb/ate*d*
mat *also* matt
mat/ador
matche*d*
mate/lot
materi/al/*ism*
mater/nity
mathemat/ic/al*ly*
matinée
matin*s*
matri/archy
matri/cide
matric/ulate*d*
matri/moni/al*ly*
mat/rixes [ices]
mat/ron*ly*

matt *also* mat
matted
mat/ter*ed*
matter-of-fact
mat/tock
mat/tress*es*
matura/tion
matur/ity
maud/lin
maul*ed*
maunder/*ing*
mauso/leum
mauve
maver/ick
mawk/ish*ly*
maxil/lary
max/imum [ima]
mayhem
mayon/naise
mayor/al*ty*
maze
ma/zurka
Mc/Carthy/*ism*
mead ↔ meed
meadow
meagre*ly*
me/ander*ed*
mean/*ness*
mean*t*
measles
measly
measure/*ment*
meatus
Mecca
mechan/ical*ly*
mechan/ism
mechan/ize

medal/*lion*
medal/*list*
meddle/*some*
media **p**
mediaeval
median
medi/ator
medic/al*ly*
medic/ament
medicin/al*ly*
medi/*cine*
medi/ocre*ly*
medi/ocrity
medita/tion
Medi/terranean
mediums *also*
    media
medleys
medul/lary
meed ↔ mead
megalo/maniac
mega/phone
mega/ton
mei/osis
melan/cholic
melan/choly
mélange
mêlée
melior/ated
melli/fluous*ly*
me/lodic
melodi/ous*ly*
melo/dramatic
melon
mem/brane
memen/to*es*
memoir

memor/abilia
memor/able
memor/andum
men/acing
mena/gerie
men/dacious*ly*
Mendel/*ian*
mendic/ant
meni/al*ly*
menin/gitis
menis/cus
men's
menses **p**
men/strual
mensura/tion
mental/*ity*
men/thol
mention/*able*
mentor
menus
meow *also*
    miaow
Mephistoph/eles
mercant/ile
mercant/ilism
mercen/ary
mercer/ized
merchand/ise
merchant/*able*
merci/less*ly*
mercuri/al*ly*
mer/curic
mere*ly*
meretri/cious*ly*
merg*ed*
meri/dian
meridi/onal

mer/ingue
meri/nos
mer/ited
merit/ori/ous*ly*
mer/maid
merri/ment
mesmer/ism
mes/quite
mess/age
messen/ger
Mes/siah
Messi/anic
messieurs **p**
meta/bolic
meta/bolism
meta/carpus
metal/*lic*
metal/*lurgy*
meta/morphosis
meta/phoric/al*ly*
meta/physic/al*ly*
meta/tarsus
met*ed*
meteor/ical*ly*
meteor/*ite*
meteoro/*logical*
meter
method/ical*ly*
Methu/selah
methyl/*ated*
meticu/lous*ly*
métier
met/onymy
metre
metric/al*ly*
metro/nome
metro/polis

metro/politan

mettle/*some*

mezzan/ine

mezzo-/

  soprano*s*

miaow *also* meow

mias/ma*l*

mica

mi/crobe

micro/cosm

micro/gram

micro/phone

micro/

  scopic/*ally*

mid/day

midget

mid/riff

mien

mignon/*ette*

mi/graine

migrat/ory

mika/do*s*

mil/dew*ed*

mile/*age*

milieu

milit/ancy

milit/ary

mili/tia

milk*i*/*ness*

mil/len/arian

millen/nium

mille/pede

millet

milli/gram

milli/litre

milli/metre

millin/ery

million/airess

mimeo/graph*ed*

mi/mesis

mim/ick*ed*

mim/ic*ry*

mimosa

min/aret

min/cing

mineral/*ogy*

mingy

mini/ature

mini/com/puter

minim/al*ly*

min/imum

minion

ministeri/al*ly*

minis/try

minor/*ity*

minuet

minus/cule

minute

minu/tia [ae]

minx

mir/acle

miracu/lous*ly*

mirage

mir/ror*ed*

mirth/ful*ly*

mis/adven/ture

mis/alli/ance

mis/anthropy

mis/apprenhen/

  sion

mis/appropri/ate

mis/behaviour

mis/calcu/lat*ed*

mis/carriage

misce/gena/tion

miscel/laneous

mis/chief

mischiev/ous*ly*

mis/conceiv*ed*

mis/construe*d*

miscre/ant

mis/demean/our

miser/ably

miser*ly*

mis/govern/*ment*

mis/guide*d*

mishap

mis/inter/pret*ed*

mis/laid

miso/gamy

miso/gynist

mis/prision

mis/pronunci/

  ation

missal

mis/shape*n*

mis/sile

mission/*ary*

mis/sive

mis/spell

mis/spelt

mis/spent

mistle/toe

mite

mitig/atory

mi/tosis

mitre

mizen *also*

  mizzen

mne/monic

moat

mobil/ity

moc/casin

mocha

mock/*ery*

modal

mod/ell*ed*

moder/ator

modern/*ness*

modi/fy*ing*

modish

modu/lar

module

mohair

Moham/me̶

  use Muhan

  mad*an*

moi/ety

moisten*ed*

mois/ture

molar

mo/lasses

molecu/lar

molli/fy*ing*

mol/lusc*an*

molten

molyb/denum

moment/*arily*

moment/*ary*

mo/ment*um*

mon/archic/al*ly*

monas/tery

mon/astic

monet/ary

money*ed*

money*s*

Mon/golia*n*

mon/goose*s*

mongrel/ize*d*
monit/or/*ial*
monkey*s*
mono/chromatic
mon/ocle
monody
mono/gamy
mono/
   gram*matic*
mono/lith*ic*
monolog/ist
mono/logue
mono/polist
mono/poly
mono/syllable
monoton/*ously*
Mon/sieur
Mon/signor
mon/soon*al*
monstros/ity
mon/strous*ly*
mont/age
mont/ane
monu/ment*al*
moose **s/p**
mope*d*
mo/poke *also*
  morepork
mo/raine
morale
moral/*ity*
morass*es*
mora/tor/ium
morbid/*ity*
mordant
mord/ent
more/over

more/pork *also*
   mopoke
morgan/atic
morgue
mori/bund
Mormon/*ism*
morn/ing
Moroc/can
mo/rocco
mor/on*ic*
morose*ly*
mor/phine
morpho/logical
Morse
morsel
mortal/*ity*
mortar
mort/gage*d*
mor/tice *also*
   mor/tise
mor/tician
mortu/ary
mo/saic
mosaick/*ing*
mos/elle
Moslem *use*
   Muslim
mosque
mos/quito*es*
mote
motel
motet
motif
motion/*less*
motive
motley
motor/ize*d*

mot/to*es*
moue
mould*y*
moult*ed*
mountain/*ous*
mourn/*ing*
mousse
mous/tache
mouth/ful*s*
movable
mucil/age
mucous **a**
mucus **n**
mud*dy*
muez/zin
mufti
Muham/mad*an*
mulat/to*s*
mul/berry
mulct*ed*
mulga
mulish/*ness*
mullah
mullet
mulliga/tawny
mul/lion
mul/lock
multi/fari/ous*ly*
mul/tiple
multi/plic/able
multi/tudin/
   ous*ly*
mum/mer*y*
mummi/fy*ing*
mundane/*ness*
muni/cipal/*ity*
muni/ficent*ly*

mural
murder/ous*ly*
murmur*ed*
musca/tel
muscle ↔
   mussel
Muscov/ite
muscular/*ity*
muscu/lature
museum
musi/cale **n**
music/all*y* **a**
musi/cian
musket/*eer*
mus/ketr*y*
Muslim
muslin
mus/quash
mussel ↔
   muscle
mus/tard
mut/able
mutil/ate*d*
mutin/eer
mutiny
mutter*ed*
mutu/al/*ity*
my/opia
myriad
myrrh
myster/ious
mystic **a/n**
mys/tify
mys/tique **n**
mythic/all*y*
mytho/logic/all*y*
myxo/matosis

N

nadir
naiad
naiv/*ety*
napalm
naphthal/*ene*
Napo/leon*ic*
nar/cissus*es*
nar/cotic
narrat/ive
nar/rator
nar/whal
nasal/*ity*
nas/cent
nasti/ness
nastur/tium
natal/*ity*
natat/ory
national/iz*ed*
nativ/ity
natural/*ism*
natural/*istic*
naught ↔
  nought
naughti/ness
naughty
naus/eat*ed*
naus/eous
nautic/al*ly*
naut/ilus
naval
nave
navel
navig/able
navig/ator

navy
Nazar/ene
Nazis*m*
Neander/thal*er*
neap
Neapol/itan
nebula **n**
neb/ular **a**
neces/sarily
neces/sary
neces/sity
necro/mancy
nectar/ine
née
ne'er
nefari/ous*ly*
negat/ive*ly*
neglect/ful*ly*
nég/ligé
neg/ligence
neg/ligible
negoti/able
negoti/ator
Ne/gress*es*
Ne/gro*es*
neighbour/*hood*
nei/ther
nem/esis
neo/lithic
neo/logism
neon
neo/phyte
nephew
neph/ritis
nepot/ism
nereid
nerv/ous*ly*

nerv/ure
nervy
nestl*ed*
nest/ling
Nether/lands
nether/most
neural
neur/algia
neur/asthenia
neuro/logist
neur/osis
neur/otic/*ally*
neuter
neutral/iz*ed*
neut/ron
newel
newt
Newton/*ian*
nexus
Niag/ara
Ni/cene
nice*ty*
niche
nick/ell*ed*
nicot/ine
niece
Nietz/sche*an*
nig/gard*ly*
nigh
night/ingale
night/marish
nihil/ism
nil
nimbus
nincom/poop
nine/teen*th*
nine*ti*/e*th*

nine*ty*
ninth*ly*
nipple
nir/vana
ni/trate
nitre
nitric
ni/trite
nitro/gen*ous*
ni/trous
Noah
nobil/ity
no/blesse oblige
noc/turnal
noc/turne
nodal
node
nodule
Noel
noggin
nog/ging*s*
nois/ily
noi/some*ly*
noisy
no/mad*ic*
nomen/clature
nomin/al*ly*
nominat/ive
nonage
nonagen/ar/ian
nonce
nonchal/ance
non/conform/ist
non/descript
non/entity
non/pareil
non/sensic/al*ly*

noodle
noose
normal/*ity*
norm*s*
Norse
north/*erly*
north/*ern*
northwester
  also nor'-
  wester
Nor/wegian
nose
nosey *use* nosy
nostal/gia
nos/tril
nos/trum
nosy
nota bene
notable
notary
nota/tion
note/worthy
notice/*able*
noti/fiable
noti/fies
noti/fy*ing*
no/tional
notori/ety
notori/ous*ly*
nougat
nought ↔
  naught
nourish/*ment*
nous
nou/veau riche
novel/*ette*
Novem/ber

novice
novici/ate *also*
  noviti/ate
nox/ious
nozzle
nu/ance
nubile
nuc/lear
nucle/ole
nuc/leus
nudist
nugat/ory
nuggety
nuis/ance
nulli/fy*ing*
numb*ed*
number/*ed*
nu/meral
numera/tion
numer/ator
numeric/al*ly*
numer/ous
num/skull
nun/cios
nun/*nery*
nup/tials
nurse/ling *also*
  nurs/ling
nursery
nur/tur*ed*
nutri/ent
nutri/ment*al*
nutri/tion*al*
nutri/tious*ly*
nutrit/ive
nut*ty*
nuzzl*ed*

nylon
nymph

O

oaf*s*
oakum
oasis [oases]
oath*s*
ob/duracy
obedi/ence
obeis/ance
obel/isk
obese
obes/ity
obey*ed*
ob/fuscat*ed*
obitu/ary
objection/*able*
object/*ive*
ob/ject*or*
ob/late
oblig/atory
oblig*ed*
obli/ging*ly*
ob/lique*ly*
ob/li/quity
ob/liter/at*ed*
ob/livion
ob/livi/ous
ob/loquy
obnox/ious*ly*
oboe*s*
oboist
ob/scene
obscen/ity

obscur/ant/*ism*
ob/scur*ed*
ob/sequies
obsequi/ous*ly*
observ/ance
observat/ory
obses/s*ion*
obsi/dian
obsoles/cent
obsol/ete
obs/tacle
obstetri/*cian*
obstin/acy
obstin/ate*ly*
ob/streper/ous*ly*
obstruct/ive*ly*
obtain/*able*
ob/trud*ed*
obtrus/ive*ly*
ob/tuse*ly*
obvi/at*ed*
obvi/ous*ly*
ocar/inas
occasion/al*ly*
Occi/dent
oc/cipital
oc/ciput
occlu/sion
occult/*ism*
occu/pancy
occupa/tion*al*
occu/pied
occu/py*ing*
oc/curr*ed*
occur/*rence*
ocean
ocelot

ochre
ochre/*ous*
ocker/*ism*
octa/go*nal*
octane
octa/roon *also*
  octo/roon
octave
octa/vos
octet (te)
Octo/ber
octo/brist
octo/genarian
octo/pu*ses*
octo/roon *also*
  octaroon
octo/syllabic
ocular/*ist*
odal/isque
odd/*ity*
ode
odious/*ness*
odium
odo/meter
odori/ferous*ly*
odor/ous*ly*
odour
Odys/sey
Oed/ipus
oeso/phagus
oestro/gen
oes/trus
offal
of/fence
offens/ive*ly*
offer*ed*
offer/tory

offici/al*ly*
offi/ciious*ly*
often
ogl*ed*
ogre*ss*
ohm
oint/ment
okay
oleagin/ous
olean/der
olfact/ory
olig/archy
oliva/ceous
olym/piad
omega
om/elette
omen
omin/ous*ly*
omis/sion
omit*ted*
omni/bus*es*
omni/potence
omni/science
omni/vorous*ly*
onan/*ism*
one/*ness*
oner/ous*ly*
one/self
onion
onomato/poeia *n*
onomato/
  poeic *a*
on/slaught
onto/geny
onto/logy
onus
onyx

oo/logist
ooz*ed*
oozy
opa/city
opal/*escent*
opal/*ine*
opaque
open/*ness*
oper/able
oper/*atic*
oper/ator
oper/etta
ophthal/mia
opiate
opinion/*ative*
opium
opos/sum *also*
  possum
op/ponent
opportun/ist
oppos*ed*
oppos/ite
oppress/ive*ly*
op/pressor
oppro/brium
opt*at*/*ive*
optic/al*ly*
opti/*cian*
optim/ism
option/al*ly*
opu/lent*ly*
opus
oracle
oracu/lar/*ity*
oral*ly*
orange/*ade*
orang-/utan

orator/*ical*
orator/ios
ora/tory
orbit/*ing*
orchard/*ist*
orches/tral
orchid
ordain*ed*
ordeal
or/derly
or/dinal
ordin/ance
ordin/ar/*ily*
ordin/ary
ord/nance
ordure
ore
oread
organ/die
organic/al*ly*
organ/*isms*
organ/ization
orgasm
orgi/astic
orgy [ies]
oriel
orient/at*ed*
ori/fices
origin/al/*ity*
origin/al*ly*
oriole
Orion
ori/sons
orlon
ormolu
ornament/al*ly*
ornate*ly*

ornitho/logy

oro/graphy

orphan/*age*

orphic

Orping/ton

or/rery

orris

ortho/centre

ortho/doxy

ortho/gonal

ortho/graphy

ortho/paedic*s*

oscil/late*d*

oscu/latory

osier

osmium

os/mosis

osse/ous

ossi/fy*ing*

ostens/ible

ostenta/tious*ly*

osteo/pathy

ostler

ostra/cize*d*

os/trich*es*

otiose

otter

Otto/man

Ouija board

ounce

ouste*d*

out/fit*ter*

out/lying

out/rage*ous*

out/rival*led*

oval

ova*ry*

ova/tion

over/all*s*

over/draught

over/rate

over/reach

over*tly*

over/ture

over/wrought

ovine

ovi/parous

ovi/positor

ovoid

ovule

ovum

owl*et*

oxid/ize*d*

Oxo/nian

oxy-acetylene

oxygen/ate*d*

oxy/moron

oyster

ozone

P

pachy/derm*at/ous*

pacific/*ally*

paci/fism

pack/age*d*

pact

pad*ded*

pad/dock

pad/lock*ed*

padre

padrone

paean

paed/erasty *also*
  ped/erasty

pagan/*ism*

pageant

pagina/tion

pagoda*s*

paid

painter*ly*

palace*s*

pal/adin

palaeo/lithic

pal/aes/tra

palan/quin

palat/able

palate ↔ pal/
  ette, pallet

pala/tial*ly*

palatin/ate

pala/vere*d*

pales/tra

pal/ette ↔
  palate, pallet

pal/frey*s*

palin/drome

paling

palis/ade*d*

palish

pal/ladium

pall*ed*

pallet ↔ palate,
  pal/ette

palli/asse

palli/ative

pallid*ly*

pallor

palm/istry

palp/able

palpit/ate*d*

palsy

paltry

pampa*s*

pampere*d*

pamphlet/*eer*

pana/cea*s*

pan/ache

pan/chromatic

pan/creas

panda

pan/demon/ium

pandere*d*

pan/egyric

panel*led*

panic*ked*

pan/ick*y*

pan/nier

panni/kin

pan/oply

pan/oramic

pansy

panta/loon

pan/technicon

pan/theon

panther/*ish*

panto/mime

pantry

papacy

papal

pa/paw

papere*d*

papier mâché

papil/la*ry*

papist

papoose

pap/rika
pa/pyrus [ri]
par
par/able
para/bola
para/chute
para/chutist
paraded
para/digm
para/disaical
para/dise
para/doxical
paraf/fin
par/agon
para/graphic
para/keet
paral/lax
par/alleled
parallelo/gram
para/lysed
para/lysis
para/meter
par/amos
par/amour
para/noia
para/pet
parapher/nalia
para/phrased
para/plegia
para/site
para/sol
para/trooper
para/typhoid
para/vane
par/celled
parcel/ling
parch/ment

pardon/able
par/doner
par/egoric
parent/age
par/ental
paren/thesis
   [ses]
paren/thetical
pa/riah
pari/etal
parish/ioner
parity
parka
par/lance
par/leyed
parlia/mentary
par/lour
par/lous
parochi/ally
parody
paroled
pa/rotid
par/oxysmal
par/quetry
parri/cide
parrotry
parry/ing
parsed
parsi/monious
parsi/mony
pars/ing
pars/ley
parson/age
partheno/
   genesis
Par/thenon
partial/ity

partial/ly
participa/tion
particip/ator
parti/ciple
particles
particular/ized
par/tisan
parti/tion
partit/ively
partnered
part/ridge
parturi/ent
parturi/tion
par/venu
pas/chal
pasha
pass/able
pas/sage
pass/ant
passé
passed v
passen/ger
passion/ately
pass/ive
passiv/ity
past a/n/prep.
paste
pastel/list
pasteur/ized
pas/tiche
pas/tille
pas/time
pas/toral a
pastor/ale n
pas/tured
pasty
patch/ouli

pate
pâté
patent
pater/familias
patern/ally
patern/ity
pater/noster
pathetic/ally
patho/genic
patho/logical
pathos
pa/tience
patin/ated
patios
patois
patri/archal
patri/cian
patri/mony
patriotic/ally
pa/trolled
patron/ess
patron/ized
pat/ronymic
patten
pat/terned
pau/city
paunchy
pauper/ized
paused
pavan also
   pavane
pave/ment
pavilioned
pawky
pay
pay/able
payee

peace/*able*
pea/cock
peak
peal*ed*
pearl*y*
peas/ant*ry*
peat*y*
pebbly
pecan
pecca/dillo*es*
pec/cant
pec/cary
pectin
pec/toral
pecula/tion
peculi/ar*ity*
pecuni/ary
ped/agogical
ped/agogue
pedal*led*
pe/dant*ic*
peddl*ed*
ped/erasty *also*
   paed/erasty
ped/estal*led*
pedes/trian
pedi/cur*ed*
pedi/gree*d*
pedi/ment
ped/lary
pedo/meter
ped/uncle
peek*ed*
peer/*age*
peer*ed*
peev/ish*ly*
pejorat/ive

Pekin/ese
pekoe
pelar/gonium
pelf
pel/ican
pe/lisse
pel/lagra
pel/let*ed*
pel/licle
pel/lucid/*ity*
pelmet
pe/lorus
pelvic
penal/iz*ed*
pen/al*ty*
pen/ance
pen/chant
pen/cill*ed*
pen/dant **n**
pendent **a**
pendu/lous*ly*
pendu/lum
pen/etrat*ed*
pen/guin
peni/cillin
pen/insula **n**
pen/insular **a**
penis
peniten/ti*ary*
pen/nant
penni/less
peno/logy
pension/*able*
pen/sion*er*
pent/acle
penta/gon*al*
penta/meter

Penta/teuch
pent/athlon
Pente/cost
pen/ultim/ate*ly*
pen/umbra*l*
penuri/ous*ly*
peon/*age*
peony
peopl*ed*
pep/per*y*
pepsin
peptic
per/ambu/lator
per/ceiv*ed*
percent/*age*
percept/*ible*
percipi/ent
percol/ator
percus/*sion*
perdi/tion
peregrin/at*ed*
per/egrine
peremp/torily
per/enni/al*ly*
perfect/*ible*
per/fervid
perfidi/ous*ly*
perfor/at*ed*
perform/*ance*
per/fum*ery*
per/functory
per/gola
peri
peri/cardia*c*
peri/gean
peri/gee
peri/helion

peril/ous*ly*
peri/meter
periodic/al*ly*
peri/patetic
peri/pheral
peri/phery
peri/phrasis
peri/scope
perish/*able*
peri/style
periton/eum
peri/wigg*ed*
peri/winkle
perjuri/ous*ly*
per/jury
perk
perk*y*
perm/alloy
perman/ency
permangan/ate
per/meabil/ity
per/meat*ed*
permiss/ible
permis/sion
permiss/ive/*ness*
per/mitt*ed*
permuta/tion
perni/cious*ly*
perora/tion
per/oxide
perpendic/ular
perpet/rator
perpetu/al*ly*
perpetu/ity
perplex/*ity*
perquis/ite
per se

per/secutor
persever/ance
per/severed
persi/flage
persim/mon
persist/ence
person/age
per/sonal
person/ality
person/alty
personi/fica/tion
person/nel
perspect/ive
per/spex
perspic/acious
perspica/city
perspicu/ity
perspic/uous
perspira/tion
perspir/atory
per/suaded
persuas/ible
persuas/ion
persuas/ive
pertain/ing
pertina/ceously
pertina/city
pertin/ently
pert/ly
perturba/tion
per/usal
per/vaded
pervas/ively
per/versely
pervers/ity
pervi/ously
pess/ary

pessim/ism
pessimist/ic/ally
pesti/cide
pesti/fer/ous
pesti/lence
pesti/len/tial
pestle
petal/led
petite
peti/tioner
petrel
petri/faction
petro/leum
petro/logy
petti/coat
pettifog/ging
pet/tish
petty
pet/ulantly
petu/nia
pew
pewter
phago/cyte
pha/langer
phalanx/es
phal/lic
phal/lus
phantas/mic
phan/tasy also
fan/tasy
phantom
Phar/aoh
Pharisa/ical
Phar/isee
pharma/ceutical
pharmaco/poeia
phar/macy

pharyn/geal
pharyn/gitis
pharynx
phase/d
pheas/ant
pheno/logy
phenol/
phthalein
phenomen/ally
phenom/enon
[ena]
phenyl
phial
phil/anderer
phil/anthropic
phil/ately
phil/harmonic
philip/pic
Philis/tine
philo/logy
philo/sopher
philo/sophical
philtre
phle/botomy
phleg/matic/ally
phlo/giston
phobia
phoenix
phone
phoneme
phoneti/cian
phoney also
phony
phonic
phono/graphy
phono/logy
phos/gene

phos/phate
phos/phine
phosphor/escent
phos/phorus
photo/genic
photo/graphic
photo/synthesis
phraseo/logy
phren/etic also
fren/etic
phreno/logy
phthisis
phylac/tery
phy/letic
phylo/geny
phylum
physic/ally
physi/cian
physi/cist
physi/ognomy
physio/logical
physio/therapy
phys/ique
pi
piano/forte
pian/ola
piano/s
piazza/s
pica
pic/ador
picar/esque
picca/ninny
pic/colos
pick/eted
pic/nicker
picot
picric

pictori/al*ly*
pictur/e*sque*
pidgin
pie/bald
piece/meal
pier
pier/cing
pier/rot
piety
pigeon
pig/*gery*
pig/ment*ary*
pigmenta/*tion*
pigmy *also*
  pygmy
pike/let
pilas/ter
pilch/ard
pil/fer*ed*
pilgrim/*age*
pil/lager*s*
pillar
pil/lion
pil/lory
pil/low*ed*
pi/lot*ed*
pimen/tos
pimper/nel
pimply
pin/afore
pince-/nez
pin/cers
pinion*ed*
pin/nace
pin/nacl*ed*
pion/eer*ed*
pious*ly*

pip/*ette*
piping
pi/quant
piqu*ed*
pirou/ett*ed*
piscat/*orial*
pis/cine
pis/tachio*s*
pistil/*lary*
pis/toll*ed*
piston
pitcher
pit/eous*ly*
pith*y*
piti/able
piti/ful
piti/less
pit/tance
pitu/itary
pity/ing*ly*
piv/ot*al*
pixie *also* pixy
pizzi/cato
plac/able
plac/ard*ed*
pla/catory
pla/cebo*s*
placen/ta [a*e or*
  a*s*]
placid/*ity*
placket
plagiar/iz*ed*
plagu*ed*
plaice
plaid
plain/*ness*
plaint/*iff*

plaint/ive*ly*
plait*ed*
planch/ette
plane
planet/*arium*
plan/gent
plank/ton
plan/tain
planta/*tion*
plaque
plasm*a*
plas/ter*er*
plasti/cine
plasti/c*ity*
plat/eaus
plat/form
platin/iz*ed*
plat/inum
platit/udin/*ous*
Pla/*tonic*
pla/toon
plat/ter
platy/puse*s*
plaudits
plaus/ible
play/wright
plaza
plea
plead*ed*
pleas/ant*ry*
pleasur/able
pleat*ed*
ple/be*ian*
pleb/iscite
plec/trum
pledg*ed*
Plei/ade*s*

plen/ary
pleni/potenti/ary
plent/eous*ly*
plenti/ful*ly*
plenum
pleth/ora
pleur/isy
plexus
pli/able
pliant*ly*
pliers
plight*ed*
plim/soll (P)
plinth
plough*ed*
plover
plum/*age*
plum/bago
plum*ber*
plummet*ed*
plung*ed*
plu/perfect
plural/*ism*
pluto/cracy
plu/*tonic*
pluto/nium
plu/vial
ply/*ing*
pneu/matic
pneu/monia
poach*er*
pock/et*ed*
podium
poem
poesy
poet/*aster*
poetic/al*ly*

po/etry
pogrom
poign/ant
poin/settia
poised
poisoned
poison/ous
poky
polar/ity
polem/ical
police/man
pol/icy
polio/myelitis
pol/ished
po/litely
polit/ical
polit/ician
polka
pol/lard
polled
pollen
pollin/ate
pollu/tion
polo
polon/aise
polter/geist
poly/chromatic
poly/gamous
poly/glottal
poly/gonal
poly/gyny
Poly/nesian
polyp
poly/theism
poly/thene
pomegran/ate
pommel

pompos/ity
pom/pously
ponce
ponder/ously
pon/tiff
ponti/fical
pon/tooned
popery
poplar
poplin
poppet
pop/ulace **n**
popu/larity
popu/lous **a**
porcel/ain
por/cine
porcu/pine
pore
porno/graphy
poros/ity
porous
por/phyry
por/poise
por/ridge
port/ability
port/able
portal
port/cullis
portent/ously
port/folios
por/tico [coes or
  cos]
por/tion
port/manteaus
portrait/ure
por/trayal
Portu/guese

poseur
posit/ively
posse
posses/sion
pos/sessor
pos/sibil/ity
pos/sum *also*
  opos/sum
post/age
poste rest/ante
poster/ior
poster/ity
post/humously
postil/ion
post meri/diem
post-/mortem
postpone/ment
post/prandial
post/script
postu/lated
pos/tured
posy
potash
potas/sium
pota/toes
potent/ate
poten/tially
potion
pot-/pourri
pot/sherd
pot/tage
pot/tery
pouf *also* pouffe
poult/iced
poultry
pouted
pov/erty

power/fully
practic/able
practic/ally
prac/tice **n**
prac/tise **v**
practi/tioner
pragmat/ically
prairies
praise/worthy
prated
prat/tling
prawns
prayers
preached
pre/amble
precar/iously
precaution/ary
preced/ence
preced/ent
pre/centor
pre/ceptor
pre/cinct
pre/cious
precip/ices
precipit/ated
precipit/ously
précis
pre/cisely
preci/sion
pre/cluded
pre/cociously
pre/conceived
pre/conception
pre/cursory
predat/ory
pre/decessor
pre/destined

pre/determine*d*
predic/able
predica/ment
predic/ate*d*
predict/*able*
pre/dic*tor*
predi/lection
pre/domin/ant*ly*
pre-/eminent*ly*
pre-/emp*tion*
preen*ed*
pre/fabric/ate*d*
pre/fac*ed*
prefat/ory
prefect/*orial*
prefer/*able*
prefer/*ence*
prefer/entiall*y*
pre/fer*red*
pre/historic
preju/dice
prejudi/cial
prelate
pre/limin/ary
pre/mature*ly*
pre/medit/ate*d*
prem/ier
premi/ère
pre/mise **v**
pre/mises **n**
premium
pre/moni/tion
pre/occupied
pre/occupy/*ing*
prepara/tion
preparat/ory

prepared/*ness*
pre/ponder/ant*ly*
preposi/tion*al*
pre/possess/*ing*
preposter/ously
pre/requisite
pre/rogat/ive
pres/age*d*
Presbyter/*ian*
presci/ent
pre/scrip*tion*
pres/ence
present/*able*
presenti/ment
preserva/tion
presid/ency
presiden/*tial*
pres/sure
pressur/ize*d*
pres/tige
prestigi/ous
presto
pre/sumably
pre/sum*ed*
presumptu/ous
pre/tence
preten/sions
preten/tious*ly*
pre/text
pret/tily
pret/zel
pre/vail*ed*
preval/ent
prevaric/ator
prevent/ive *also*
  prevent*at*/ive
pre/view*ed*

previ/ous*ly*
prey*ed*
price/*less*
prick*ly*
prie-/dieu
priest*ly*
priggish/*ness*
prima donna
prima facie
pri/macy
primal
prim/arily
prim/ate
primer
prim/eval
primit/ive*ly*
primo/geniture
prim/ordi/all*y*
prim/ula
primus
prin/cesses
princip/al*ity*
princip/all*y*
prin/ciples
prior/*ity*
pris/m*atic*
prisoner
pris/tine
priv/acy
privat/*eer*
privet
privil/ege*d*
privy
probabil/ity
prob/ably
pro/bate
proba/tion*ary*

prob/ity
problem/*atic*
probos/cis
pro/cedure
pro/ceed*ed*
proceed/ing*s*
proces/sion*al*
pro/claim*ed*
proclama/tion
procliv/ity
procrastin/ate*d*
procre/ative
proc/tor
procur/ator
pro/cur*ed*
prodig/al*ity*
prodigi/ous*ly*
prod/igy
producti*v*/*ity*
pro/fan*ed*
profan/ity
profes/sion*al*
profession/all*y*
professor/iall*y*
prof/fer*ed*
profi/ciency
pro/file
profit/*able*
prof/ite*d*
profit/*eer*
proflig/acy
pro/found*ly*
profund/ity
pro/fuse*ly*
pro/genitor
pro/geny
prognath/ous

59

pro/gnosis
prognostic/ated
pro/gramm/able
pro/gram also
  pro/gramme
progress/ively
prohibi/tion
project/ile
pro/jection
pro/jector
pro/lapse
pro/lapsus
prolet/ariat
prolifi/city
prolix/ity
pro/logue
promenaded
promin/ently
promiscu/ously
promiscu/ity
prom/ised
promis/sory
promon/tory
pro/moter
promo/tion
promul/gated
prone
pro/nominal
pro/noun
pronounce/ment
pro/nunci/ation
pro/paedeutic
propa/ganda
propag/ator
propel/lant n
pro/pelled
propel/lent a

propel/ler
propen/sity
properly
prop/erty
proph/ecy n
proph/esy v
prophet/ic/ally
pro/phylactic
pro/phylaxis
propin/quity
propiti/atory
pro/pitiously
pro/ponent
pro/portional
pro/posal
proposi/tional
propri/etary
propri/etor
propri/ety
pro/pulsion
pro/roga/tion
pro/rogued
prosaic/ally
proscen/ium
pro/scribed
prose
prosecu/tion
prosecu/tor
pros/elyte
pro/sit
pros/ody
pro/spector
pro/spectus
prosper/ity
prosper/ously
pro/state
pros/thesis [ses]

prosti/tute
prot/agon/ist
pro/tean
pro/tection
pro/tector/ate
pro/tégé
pro/tein
protest/ant (P)
pro/thesis
proto/col
proton
proto/plasmic
proto/type
proto/zoa
pro/tractor
pro/trudent
pro/tuber/ant
provable
proven/ance
prov/ender
proverbi/ally
provid/ence
providen/tial
provincial/ism
provision/ally
pro/visos
provoca/tion
provocat/ively
pro/voked
prov/ost
prow/ess
prowler
proxim/ate
proxim/ity
proxy [xies]
pruden/tially
prudishly

pruri/ency
prussic
prying
psalm/ist
psal/tery
pseud/onymous
psittac/osis
psyche
psychi/atric
psychi/atrist
psychi/atry
psych/ical
psycho/logical
psycho/logist
psycho/logy
psych/osis
ptar/migan
ptero/dactyl
Ptolem/aic
pto/maine
pu/berty
pubes/cence
pub/lican
publi/cist
publi/city
pub/licly
puckered
puer/ile
puer/peral
puffin
pugil/istic
pugna/ciously
puis/sant
pulchrit/ude
puling
pulleys
pulmon/ary

pulpit
puls/atory
pulsed
pulver/ized
puma
pumice
pummel*led*
pumper/nickel
pump/kin
pun/cheon
punc/tilio
punctili/ous*ly*
punctu/al*ity*
punctu/ation
punc/tured
pundit
pun/gent*ly*
punish/*able*
punit/ive*ly*
punnet
puny
pupa*e*
pupal
pupil
pup/pet*ry*
purchas/able
purée
purgat/ive
purgat/ory
purged
puri/fy*ing*
purit/anic/al*ly*
purity
purled
pur/lieu*s*
pur/loin*ed*
purple

pur/ported
pur/pose*ly*
purpos/ive*ly*
purred
purser
pursu/ant
pursued
pursu/ing
pur/suit
pursy
puru/lent
pur/veyor
pur/view
pus
pusil/lanim/ity
pusil/lanim/ous
pus/tule
putat/ive
putre/faction
putre/fy*ing*
putres/cent
putrid
putsch
putted
puttee
putty/*ing*
puzzle/*ment*
pygmy *also*
   pigmy
pyjamas
pylon
pyl/orus
pyram/id*al*
pyre
Pyren/ees
pyr/ethrum
pyr/idine

pyrite*s*
pyro/technic*al*
Pyr/rhic
Pythag/oras
Pythagor/ean
python/*ess*

Q

quad/rangle
quad/rant
quad/ratic
quadrenni/al*ly*
quadri/lateral
quad/rille
quadru/ped
quadru/ped*al*
quadru/ple*t*
quaff*ed*
quag/mire
quail*ed*
quaint*ly*
quaker (Q)
quali/fica/tion
quali/fy*ing*
qualitat/ive*ly*
qualm
quan/dary
quanti/fy*ing*
quantitat/ive
quantum [ta]
quarant/ine*d*
quar/rel*led*
quarry/*ing*
quar/tet
quart/ile

quarto*s*
quartz
quash*ed*
quat/rain
qua/very
quay
queasi/ness
queen*ly*
queer*ly*
quell*ed*
quench/*able*
queru/lous*ly*
query/*ing*
quest
question/*able*
question/*naire*
queue*d*
queu/ing
quies/cent
qui/etened
qui/etus
quiff
quilt*ed*
quin/ine
quinsy
quint/ain
quin/tal
quint/essence
quin/tet
quintu/ple*t*
quip*ped*
quire
quirk
quis/ling
quite
quit/*tance*
quit*ted*

quiver*ed*

quix/otic

quizz*ed*

quoin

quoit

quon/dam

quorum

quota

quota/tion

quot*ed*

quoth

quoti/dian

quo/tient

R

rabbet/*ing*

rabbin/*ical*

rabbit/*ing*

rabid*ly*

ra/bies

rac/coon *also*
  racoon

racial/*ism*

racket *also*
  racquet

racket/*eer*

racon/teur

racoon *also* rac/
  coon

racquet *also*
  racket

racy

radar

radi/al*ly*

radi/ant*ly*

radi/ation

radi/ator

radic/al*ly*

rad/icle

radio*ed*

radi/ologist

radio*s*

radish*es*

radius [dii]

raffia

raff/ish

raffle

rag/amuffin

rag*ed*

raging

raglan

ragout

rail/*lery*

rai/ment

rain ↔ reign,
  rein

rais*ed*

raisin

raison d'être

raja *also* rajah

rakish

rally/*ing*

ram/ekin

rami/fica/tion

ram/pag*ed*

ram/pag*eous*

ramp/ant

ram/part

rancid/*ity*

rancor/ous*ly*

ran/cour

random/*ness*

rankl*ed*

ran/sack*ed*

ransom*ed*

ranun/culus

Raphael/*esque*

rapid/*ity*

rapier

rapine

rap/port

rap/proche/ment

rapt

raptur/ous*ly*

rara avis

rarebit

rar/efaction

rarefy/*ing*

rarity

rascal/*ity*

rasp/berry

ratchet/*ing*

rate/*able*

rati/fying

ratiocin/at*ed*

ration/ale

rational/*ism*

rational/*ize*

ratio*s*

ratoon*ed*

rattan

rauc/ous*ly*

ravag*ed*

ravel*led*

raven/ous*ly*

ra/vin*ed*

ravish/*ing*

rayon

raz*ed*

razor

react/ant*s*

re/action/*ary*

react/iv/at*ed*

read/*able*

read/ily

re/afforest*ed*

real/iz*ed*

real/*ism*

real/istic/*ally*

real*ly*

realm

real/politik

real/tor

re/alty

ream

re/appraisal

rear*ed*

re/arrange/*ment*

reason/*able*

re/assurance

rebat*ed*

re/bel*led*

rebel*li/ous*

rebuk*ed*

rebut/*tal*

recalcit/rant*ly*

re/capitu/lat*ed*

reced*ed*

re/ceipt*ed*

re/ceiv/able

re/ceiver

re/cency

re/cent*ly*

recept/acle

recep/tion

receptiv/ity

recess*ed*
reces/sion*al*
recess/*ive*
recher/ché
recidiv/*ist*
recipe
recipi/*ent*
reciproc/al*ly*
reci/procity
re/cital
recita/*tion*
reck/less*ly*
reckon*ed*
re/claim*ed*
reclama/*tion*
re/clining
re/cluse
recogniz/ab*ly*
recogniz/*ance*
re/coil*ed*
recol/lec*tion*
recommend/ *able*
recom/pens*ed*
recon/cil*ed*
reconcili/*ation*
recon/dite
reconnais/ sance
recon/noitr*ed*
re/course
recov/ery
recre/ant
recre/at*ed*
recre/ation
recrimin/atory
recrudes/c*ence*

re/cruit*ed*
rect/angle
rect/angular
recti/fiable
recti/linear
rectit/ude
rect/ory
rectum
recum/bent
recuper/at*ed*
re/curr*ed*
recur/*rence*
recus/ant
re/deem*er*
redemp/tion
redol/ent
redoubt/*able*
re/ducible
redund/ancy
re-echo*ed*
reed*y*
reef*s*
reek*ed*
reel*ed*
refect/ory
refer/ee*d*
refer/*ence*
refer/endum
re/ferr*ed*
re/finer*y*
re/flec*tion* also
  re/flexion
re/flector
reflex/*ible*
re/flexion also
  re/flection
reforma/*tion*

reformat/*ory*
refract/*ory*
re/frain*ed*
refriger/ator
refuel/*led*
refu/gee
re/fusal
re/futable
refut*ed*
regal*ed*
regalia
reg/al*ly*
regard/*less*
re/gatta*s*
re/gency
regener/ator
regi/cide
regime *also*
  régime
regi/men
regi/ment*al*
region/al*ly*
regis/ter*ed*
regis/trar
regis/try
regress/*ive*
regret/*tably*
re/gret*ted*
regu/larity
regu/lation*s*
regu/lator
re/gurgit/at*ed*
re/habilit/at*ed*
re/habilita/tion
re/hearsal
Reichs/*tag*
reify/*ing*

reign ↔ rain,
  rein
re/imburs*ed*
re/incarn/at*ed*
rein ↔ rain,
  reign
rein/deer
re/inforce/*ment*
re/issu*ed*
re/iter/at*ed*
reject/*able*
re/joicing
rejuven/at*ed*
re/laps*ed*
rela/tion*al*
rela/tion/*ship*
relativ/ity
relaxa/*tion*
relay*ed*
re/leas*ed*
releg/at*ed*
relent/*less*
relev/ance
relev/ant*ly*
reli/ab*ly*
reli/ance
relic
relict
relief
re/liev*ed*
reli/gious*ly*
relin/quish*ed*
rel/iquary
relish*ed*
reluct/ance
rely/*ing*
remain/*der*

63

remark/*able*	re/occupy/*ing*	re/prise	res/istor
remedi/able	rep *also* repp	reproach/*fully*	re/soluble
remedi/*ally*	repaid	reprob/ate	resol/*utely*
remedy/*ing*	repair/*able*	re/proof	resolu/tion
remem/ber*ed*	repar/able	re/proving*ly*	re/solv*ent*
remem/brance	repara/tion	rep/tile	reson/ance
remin/isce	repar/tee	rep/tilian	reson/ant
reminis/*cence*	re/patri/at*ed*	repub/lic*an*	reson/ator
remiss/*ness*	repay	repudi/at*ed*	re/sorp/tion
remit/*tance*	repeal*ed*	repug/*nance*	resort*ed*
re/mitt*ed*	repeat/*able*	repuls/*ively*	resource/*fully*
rem/nant	repeat/*edly*	reput/*ably*	respect/*able*
remon/strance	repêch/*age*	re/quest*ed*	respect/*fully*
remorse/*lessly*	re/pell*ed*	re/quiem	respect/*ively*
remote*ly*	repel/*lent*	require/*ment*	respira/tion
re/movable	repent/*ant*	requi/site	respir/atory
re/moval	repercus/sion	requisi/tion*ed*	resplen/dent
remuner/at*ed*	reper/toire	re/quit*ed*	respond/*ent*
remunera/tion	reper/tory	res/cind*ed*	re/sponse
renais/sance (R)	repeti/tion	res/cu*ed*	respons/ibil/ity
renal	repetit/*ively*	rescu/*ing*	respons/ible
renas/cent	replen/ish*ed*	re/search*er*	respons/ory
rencontre	re/plete	resemb/lance	restaur/ant
render*ed*	replic/at*ed*	resent/*fully*	restaurat/eur
rendez/vous	reply/*ing*	reserva/tion	restitu/tion
rendi/tion	repose/*ful*	reser/voir	rest/*ively*
reneg/ade	reposit/ory	resid/*ence*	restora/tion
reneg*ed also*	reposses/s*ion*	residen/*tial*	re/strai*nt*
renegu*ed*	repp *also* rep	residu/*ally*	restrict/*ively*
renew/*able*	repre/hend*ed*	res/idue	result/*ant*
renew*al*	reprehens/ible	re/siduum	resump/tion
rennet	representa/tion	resigna/tion	resur/gent
re/nounc*ed*	representat/*ive*	re/sili/*ently*	resur/rection
renov/ator	repress/*ively*	resin/*ous*	resuscit/at*ed*
re/nown*ed*	re/priev*ed*	resist/*ance*	retail*er*
renunci/ation	reprim/and*ed*	resist/*ibil/ity*	retain*ed*
renunci/atory	re/prisal	resistiv/*ity*	retali/atory

retarda/*tion*

retch*ed*

retent/ive*ly*

reti/cence

reticu/lat*ed*

ret/icule

ret/inal

ret/inue

re/tiral

retire/*ment*

retort*ed*

retract/*able*

retribu/tion

retribu/tive

re/triev*er*

retro/activ*e*

retro/ced*ed*

retro/cession

retro/grade

retrogress/ive*ly*

retro/spective*ly*

re/union

re/unit*ed*

reveal*ed*

re/veille

revela/tion

revel/*ling*

rev/elry

revenge/*ful*

rev/enue

reverber/ate*d*

rever/enc*ed*

rever/end

rever/ent*ial*

rev/erie

re/versal

re/vers*ed*

revers/ible

rever/sion*ary*

revert/*ible*

review*ed*

revision/*ary*

revival/*ist*

re/vivi/fy*ing*

revoca/tion

revok*ed*

revolu/tion/*ary*

re/volver

revue

revul/sion

reward*ed*

rhapsod/iz*ed*

rhap/sody

rhea

rhe/nium

rheo/stat

rhesus

rhet/oric*al*

rhetor/ic*ian*

rheum*at*/ism

Rhine

rhino/ceros*es*

rhiz/ome

rho/dium

rhodo/dendron

rhomb/oid*al*

rhom/bus

rhu/barb

rhym*ed*

rhym/*ing*

rhyth/m*ic*

rib/ald*ry*

rib/bon*ed*

rick *also* wrick

rick/ety

rick/sha *also*
   rick/shaw

rico/chet*ed*

riddl*ed*

ridgy

ridi/cul*ed*

ridicu/lous*ly*

Ries/ling

rife

riff-raff

rifl*ed*

rift

rig*ged*

right/eous/*ness*

rigid/*ity*

rigmar/ole

rigor mor/tis

rigor/ous*ly*

rigour

rime

ring/lets

rins*ed*

riot/*ously*

ri/post*ed*

rip*ped*

ripply

ris/ibil/ity

ris/ible

ris/otto

risqué

ris/sole

rite*s*

ritual/*istic*

ri/vall*ed*

ri/valry

river/*ain*

river/*ine*

riv/et*ed*

rivet*er*

rivu/let

roach

road/*ster*

roam*ed*

roan

roast*ed*

rob/*bery*

robin

robot

robust*ly*

rock/et*ed*

rococo

rodent

rodeo*s*

roe

roent/gen **n**

rogue

roguish

roister/*ing*

role

rollick/*ing*

roly-/poly

Roman

roman/cer

Roman/*esque*

Roma/nia*n*

Ro/man*ic*

romantic/*ally*

ron/deau **s**

rondel

rondo*s*

Rönt/gen

rood

roof*s*

rook/*ery*
ros/aceous
rosar/ian
rosary
roseate
ros/ette
ros/ily
roster*ed*
rost/rum
rosy
rotary
rota/tion
ro/tator
rote
rotor
rotten/*ness*
ro/tunda
rotund/*ity*
rouble
roué
rouge*d*
rough/*age*
roul/ade
roul/ette
round/elay
roust/about
rouse*d*
rout **n/v**
route
routine
rowel*led*
row/lock
royal/*ist*
roy/al*ty*
rub/*bery*
rub/bish
rubble

Rubi/con
rubi/cund
rubric
ruche*d*
ruck/sack
rudder/*less*
rudiment/
   ary
rue/ful*ly*
ruff
ruf/fian
ruffle*d*
rugby (R)
rugged
ruin/*ously*
ruler
rumba
rumble*d*
rumbus/tious
rumin/ant
rum/mage*d*
rumoure*d*
rumpus
rune
runic
runnel
rupee
rup/ture*d*
rural
ruse
russet
Rus/sia*n*
rustic/ate*d*
rustle*d*
ruta/baga
ruth/less/*ness*
rut*ted*

rye
ryot

S

sabbat/arian
sabbat/ical
Sabine
sable
sabot/age*d*
sabot/eur
sabre
sac
sacchar/ine
sacer/dotal
sachet
sack
sacral
sacrament/al*ly*
sacred/*ness*
sacri/fice*d*
sacri/ficial
sacrilege
sacri/legious
sac/risty
sacro/sanct
sacrum
sad/den*ed*
saddle*d*
sadism
safari
safe/guard
safe*ty*
saf/flower
saf/fron
saga/cious*ly*

saga*s*
sage*ly*
saggy
Sagit/tarius
sago*s*
Sahara
sahib (S)
sailo*r*
saint*li*/*ness*
saki
sal vola/tile
salaame*d*
sala/cious*ly*
salad
sala/mander
salami
salary
sale
sale/able
salicyl/ate
sali/ent
sali/fer/ous
saline
salin/ity
saliv/ate*d*
sallow
sally/*ing*
salmon
salon
saloon
saltat/ory
salt/petre
salu/brious
saluki
salut/ary
saluta/tion
sal/vage

sal/varsan (S)
salva/tion
salved
salver
salvos
Samar/itan
samba
Samoan
samo/var
Sam/oyed
sampan
sampled
sam/urai
sanat/orium
sancti/fying
sanctimoni/
    ously
sanc/tions
sanc/tity
sanctu/ary
sandal/wood
sand/wiches
sang/froid
sanguin/ary
san/guine
sanit/ary
san/ity
san/serif
Sans/krit
Santa Claus
sapid
sapi/ently
sap/ling
sapo/naceous
sap/phire
sara/band
sar/casm

sar/coma
sarco/phagus
sar/dine
sardonic/ally
sar/gassoes
sari
sarong
sarsa/parilla
sartor/ially
sassa/fras
Sassen/ach
satanic/ally
satchel
sated
satel/lite
sati/able
satiated
sati/ety
satiny
satire
satir/ical
satis/fact/ory
satis/fying
satrap
satur/ated
Satur/day
satur/nalian
satur/nine
satyr
sauce
saucer
sauci/est
saucy
sauer/kraut
saun/tered
saur/ian
saus/age

sauté
Sau/terne
savable
sav/agery
savan/na also
    savan/nah
sav/ant
sav/eloy
sa/viour
savoir faire
sa/voury
sawyer
saxi/frage
saxophone
scab/bard
sca/bies
scabi/ous
scaffold/ing
scalars
scalded
sca/lene
scal/loped also
    scolloped
scally/wag
scalped
scal/pel
scaly
scandal/ously
Scandin/avian
scan/ner
scan/sion
scanti/est
scant/ling
scanty
scape/goat
scapu/lar
scarab

scarce/ly
scarcity
scared
scarfs also
    scarves
scari/fier
scar/ious
scarlat/ina
scar/let
scarp
scarred
scathe/less
scath/ing
scato/logy
scav/enged
scen/arios
scenery
scenic/ally
scented
sceptic/ally
sceptre
sched/uled
schem/atic
schemed
scherzos
schil/ling
schis/matic
schiz/oid
schizo/phrenia
schmaltz
schnapps
schnauzer
scholar/ship
scholastic/ally
schooner
scia/graphy
sciat/ica

sci/ence
scient/ific
scim/itar
scintil/lated
scion
scis/sors
scler/oid
scler/osis
scol/loped *also*
   scal/loped
sconce
scone
scooter
scorched
scorn/fully
scor/pion
Scotch
scotia
Scot/tish
scoundrelly
scoured
scourged
scouting
scow
scowled
scrabbled
scraggi/ness
scraped
scrappy
scrawled
scrawny
screechy
screed
screened
scribbled
scribe
scrim/mage

scrip
script
scrip/tural
scriv/ener
scrof/ula
scroll
scro/tum [ta]
scrounger
scrubby
scrum/mage
scruple
scrupu/lously
scrutin/eer
scud/ding
scuffled
sculler
scull/ery
scullion
sculptor
sculp/ture
scummy
scup/pered
scurfy
scurril/ously
scur/viest
scurvy
scut/cheon *also*
   escut/cheon
scuttled
scythed
seam/stress *also*
   sempstress
seamy
seance
searched
seared
season/able

season/ally
seba/ceous
seca/teurs
seceded
seces/sion
seclu/sion
second/ary
se/crecy
secret/aire
secret/ariat
secret/ary
se/creted
sectar/ian
sectional
sector
secu/lar
secured
secur/ity
sedan
sedately
sedat/ive
sedent/ary
sedi/ment/ary
sedi/tiously
seduced
sedu/lously
seedi/ness
seemly
seeped
seer
seer/sucker
seethed
segment/ary
segreg/ated
seigneur/ial
seignior/ial
seine

seis/mic
seismo/graph
seized
seiz/ure
seldom
select/ivity
se/lector
selen/ium
selfish/ness
sel/vage *also*
   selvedge
semanti/cist
sema/phored
semb/lance
semen
semes/ter
semi/breve
semi/circle
sem/inal
semin/ary
semi/otic
Semite
Sem/itic
semo/lina
semp/stress *also*
   seam/stress
senate
senat/orial
sendal
senes/cent
senes/chal
senile
senil/ity
senior/ity
senna
sennet
señora

señor/*ita*
sensa/tional/*ism*
sense/less/*ness*
sens/ibil/*ity*
sens/ible
sensit/ive
sensit/ivity
sensor/ium
sens/ory
sensu/al*ity*
sen/tence
senten/tious*ly*
sen/tient
sentiment/al*ly*
sen/tinel
sentry
sepal
separ/ate*ly*
separa/tion
separ/ator
sepia
sepoy
sepsis
Septem/ber
septi/caemia
septic/al*ly*
septua/genarian
septum
sepul/chral*ly*
sep/ulchre
sepul/ture
sequel
se/quence
sequen/tial*ly*
seques/ter*ed*
sequin
se/quoia

se/raglio*s*
ser/aph*ic*
sere
seren/ade*d*
seren/ata
seren/dipity
serene*ly*
serf/*dom*
serge
ser/geant
serial/ize*d*
seri/ate*d*
seri/culture
series **s**/**p**
serif
ser/ious*ly*
sermon/ize*d*
serpent/*ine*
ser/rate*d*
ser/ried
serum
ser/vant
serv/*ery*
service/*able*
servi/ette
serv/ile*ly*
serv/ility
ses/ame
sesam/oid
ses/sional
ses/terce
sestet *also*
   sextet
seta/ceous
settee
settle/*ment*
sev/enth

seventi/*eth*
sever/al*ly*
sever/*ance*
severe*ly*
sever/ity
sewage
sewer/*age*
sewn
sexa/genarian
sex/tant
sextet *also*
   sestet
sexton
sexu/al*ly*
shab/bily
shadi/ness
shaggy
shah
Shake/spear/ian
shaki/ness
shaky
shale
shal/lop
shal/lot
shal/low
shambles
shameful/*ness*
sham*med*
sham/pooe*d*
shang/haie*d*
shan/tung
shapeli/*ness*
shape*ly*
shat/tere*d*
shawl
sheaf [sheaves]
shear*er*

sheath **n**
sheath*ed* **v**
sheen
sheer
sheikh
sheila (S)
shekel
shel/lacke*d*
shelter/*less*
shel/ving
shenan/igan*s*
shep/herde*d*
sher/bet
sher/iff
Sherpa
Shet/land
shibbol/eth
shield*ed*
shi/est *also*
   shy/*est*
shille/lagh
shilly-/shally
shily *also* shyly
shim/mere*d*
shingly
shinier
shining
Shinto/*ism*
shiny
shipp*ed*
shirk*ed*
shirr/*ing*
shirt/*less*
shoal
shoddy
shoe/*ing*
shogun/*ate*

shorn

short/*age*

short/en*ed*

shoul/der*ed*

shovel*led*

shrap/nel

shred*ded*

shrewd*ly*

shrewish/*ness*

shriek*ed*

shrill*y*

shrink/*age*

shrivel*led*

shriv*en*

shroud*ed*

shrub/*bery*

shudder/*ing*

shun*ned*

shut/tl*ed*

shy*er also* shier

shy/*est also* shi/
est

Shy/lock

shy*ly also* shily

shy/ster

Siam/*ese*

Siber/*ian*

sibil/ant

sib/ling

sibyl/*line*

sic

Sicil/ian

sickle

sick*li/ness*

sick*ly*

sider/eal

siding

sidl*ed*

siege

sierra

siesta

siev*ed*

sigh/*ing*

sight*ed*

sign*ed*

signal/iz*ed*

signal*led*

signat/ory

signa/ture

signet

signific/ance

Sikh

silage

si/lenc*er*

silhou/ett*ed*

silic/at*ed*

sil/icon

silla/bub *also*
    sylla/bub

silli/ness

silos

silt*ed*

silvan *also*
    sylvan

silvi/culture *also*
    sylvi/culture

sim/ian

simil/ar*ity*

simil*es*

simil/itude

simmer/*ing*

simony

simoom

simple/*ton*

sim/plicity

simpli/fy*ing*

simu/lat*ed*

simultan/eity

simul/taneous*ly*

sin/cere*ly*

sincer/ity

sine

sine/cure

sinewy

singe/*ing*

sing/*ing*

Sing/hal/ese *also*
    Sin/halese

singly

singular/*ity*

sinis/ter

sinis/tral

Sinn Fein

sino/logue

sinter

sinu/osity

sinu/ous*ly*

sinus*es*

Sioux **s/p**

siphon*ed*

sippet

siren

sir/loin

siroc/cos

sisal

sissy *also* cissy

sisy/phean (S)

site

situ/at*ed*

situ/ation

sixth*ly*

six/*tieth*

size/*able*

sizz/ling

skein

skel/eton

sker/rick

sketch/*ily*

skewer

ski/*ing*

skil/ful*ly*

skillet

skill-/*less*

skip/per*ed*

skip/p*ing*

skirl*ed*

skirmish/*ing*

skit/tish

skittl*ed*

skua

skul/duggery

skulk/ing*ly*

skulk*ed*

skull

slalom

slander/ous*ly*

slat/tern*ly*

slaty

slaugh/ter*er*

slavish*ly*

sleazy

sleek*ly*

sleety

sleigh

sleight-/of-/hand

sleuth-/hound

slew*ed*

slily *also* sly*ly*

slimed
sli/mier
slim/*ming*
slimy
slip/*pery*
sliver
slob/*bery*
sloe
slogan
slop*pi*/*est*
slop*py*
sloth/ful*ly*
slouched
sloughed
slovenli/*ness*
slug/*gish*
sluiced
slum/bered
slumber/ous*ly*
slur*ry*
slyer
sly*ly also* slily
sly/*ness*
smatter/*ing*
smeared
smegma
smirched
smirked
smite
smither/eens
smith*y*
smitten
smoko*s*
smoky
smoothed
smorgas/bord
smouldered

smudgi/*ness*
smudgy
smug/gler
snaky
snared
sneak/*ily*
sneer/*ingly*
sneezed
snig/gered
snip/*pet*
snivel*led*
snobbish/*ness*
snood
snooker
snoozed
snor/kel
snout
snug/*gery*
soar/*ing*
sober*ly*
sobri/ety
sobri/quet
soc/cer
soci/able
socializa/*tion*
social/*ism*
societ/ies
soci/ety
sociologic/al*ly*
sock/eted
soda
sodal/ity
sod/den
sodium
sodom/*ite*
sofa
soirée

so/journed
solaced
solar/*ium*
soldered
sol/dier*ly*
sole*ly*
sol/ecism
solem/n*ity*
solemn/*ness*
solen/oid
so/licitor
solicit/ude
solid/*arity*
sol/idus
soli/loquy [ies]
soli/loquized
solips/ism
solit/aire
solit/ary
solit/ude
solo/*ist*
solo*s*
sol/stice
solubil/ity
sol/uble
solute
solu/tion
solv/ency
solv/ent
so/ma*tic*
sombre*ly*
som/brero*s*
somer/sault *also*
    summer/sault
Somer/set
somnambu/lism
somno/lent

sonant
sonar
sonata
sonat/ina
sonic
sonnet/*eer*
sonor/ous*ly*
sooner
sooth/sayer
soothed
sophistic/ated
sopho/more
soporific/al*ly*
sop/ranos
sor/cerer
sordid*ly*
sor/ghum
so/rites
soroptim/ist
soror/ity
sorrel
sorrow/ful*ly*
sorties
sotto voce
soufflé
soughed
sought
soul/ful*ly*
source
sour/dough
soused
sou/tane
south/*erly*
south/*ern*
southwester
    also sou'-
    wester

sou/venir
sover/eign*ty*
Soviet
sow*ing*
soya
spa
spacious
spa/ghetti
span/drel
spangle*d*
Span/iard
span/iel
Span/ish
span/ner
sparing*ly*
sparkle*d*
spar/ring
spar/row
sparse/*ly*
Spar/ta*n*
spas/mo*dic*
spas/tic
spati/ali*ty*
spatu/la*te*
spawne*d*
spaye*d*
special/*ist*
speci/ali*ty*
special/iza*/tion*
special*ty*
specie
species **s/p**
speci/fic*ally*
speci/fica*/tion*
speci/men
spe/cious*ly*
spec/tacle*s*

spectacu/lar*ly*
spec/tator
spec/tral
spectre
spectro/scope
spec/trum
specu/late*d*
speech/*less*
speedo/*meter*
spele/ologist
spelle*d* also
   spelt
sperma/*ceti*
spermato/*zoa*
spewe*d*
sphag/num [na]
sphen/oid
sphere
spher/ical
sphinc/ter*al*
sphinx
spic/*ate*
spicy
spidery
spiel
spigot
spike/nard
spin/ach
spinal
spindly
spine/*less*
spin/naker
spin/ney
spinster/*hood*
spiny
spir/acle
spiralle*d*

spire
spir/ite*d*
spiritual/*ism*
spirte*d* also
   spurte*d*
spit/*toon*
splaye*d*
spleen
splen/did*ly*
splend/our
splen/etic
splin/tery
splut/tere*d*
spoke
spoli/ation
spon/daic
spon/dee
sponge*d*
spongi/ness
spong/ing
spongy
spon/sore*d*
spon/taneity
spon/taneous*ly*
spoon/ful*s*
spoor
spor/adic
spore
spor/ran
spor/ule
spouse
sprawle*d*
spraye*d*
spree
sprightly ↔
   spritely
spring/bok

sprite **n**
sprocket
spruce*d*
spry*er*
spue*d* use
   spewe*d*
spume
spurre*d*
spuri/ous*ly*
spurne*d*
spur/rier
spurte*d* also
   spirte*d*
sput/nik
sputum
squab
squabble*d*
squad/*ron*
squalid
squal*ly*
squalor
squan/dere*r*
square*d*
squarish
squat*ted*
squaw
squawke*d*
squeake*d*
squeale*d*
squeam/ish*ly*
squeeze*d*
squelchy
squibbe*d*
squid
squinte*d*
squire/archy
squirme*d*

squir/rel
squirt/ed
stabil/ized
stabled
stac/cato
sta/dium
stag/gered
stag/nant
stag/nated
stagi/ness
stagey *also*
   stagy
staid
stair/case
staked
stalac/tite
stalag/mite
stale/mate
stalky
stal/lion
stal/wart
stamen
stam/ina
stam/mered
stam/peded
stance
stanched ↔
   staunched
stan/chioned
standard/iza/
   tion
standard/ized
stan/nic
stan/zaic
staphylo/coccus
stapled
star/board

starchy
stark/ness
star/ling
starry
start/ling
star/vation
starve/ling
static/ally
station/ary
station/ery
statisti/cian
statu/ary
statu/esque
stat/ure
status
stat/ute
statut/ory
staunched ↔
   stanched
steadfast/ness
steadi/ness
steady/ing
steal
stealth/ily
steami/est
steamy
steeli/ness
steely
steeple/chase
steer/age
stel/lar
stel/lated
stellu/lar
stemmed
sten/cilled
steno/grapher
stentor/ian

stephan/otis
step/ney
steppes
stereo/phonic
ster/eos
stereo/typed
ster/ile
steril/ity
steril/ize
ster/ling
stern/ness
sternum
stertor/ously
stetho/scope
stet/son
steve/dore
steward/ess
sthenic
stick/ler
stifle
stifling
stigmat/ized
stile
stil/ettos
stillborn
still/ness
stilted
stilus *use* stylus
stimu/lant
stimu/lus [li]
stingi/ness
stingy
stink/ard
stipendi/ary
stippled
stipu/lation
stir/rer

stir/ringly
stir/rup
stitched
stoat
stock/aded
stock/inet
stodgi/ness
stodgy
sto/icism
stolen
stolid/ity
stomachic
stonk/ered
stony-/hearted
stooped
stopped
stor/age
storey ↔ story
stor/eyed ↔
   stor/ied
storeys ↔ stor/
   ies
stor/ies ↔
   storeys
stork
story ↔ storey
stoup
stow/age
stow/away
straightened
strait/jacket
strait/laced
straits
strangely
strangle/hold
strangu/lated
strata **p**

strata/gem
strategic/*ally*
strat/egy
strath
strati/*fying*
strato-/cumulus
strato/sphere
stratum [ta]
stratus
straw/berry
streaki/*ness*
streaky
stream*ed*
strengthen*ed*
strenu/*ously*
strepto/coccus
stress
stretch*ed*
strew*n*
stri/*ately*
stricken
strict*ure*
stri/dent*ly*
strife
Strine
strin/gent*ly*
stripe*d*
strip/*ling*
strip*ped*
stripy
stron/tium
strop*ped*
structur/al*ly*
strug/gling
strum/pet
strut*ted*
strych/nine

stub/bly
stubborn/*ness*
stuc/co*es*
stu/dio*s*
studi/*ously*
study/*ing*
stulti/*fying*
stupefy/*ing*
stupen/dous*ly*
stu/pid/*ity*
stupor
stur/dily
stur/geon
stut/ter*ed*
style
styl/ist*ic*
styl/ite
styl/iz*ed*
stylus
sty/mie*d*
styp/tic
sua/sion
suave*ly*
suav/ity
subal/tern
sub/conscious
sub/due*d*
subdu/ing
subject/ive*ly*
subjug/at*ed*
subjunct/ive*ly*
sublim/at*ed*
sublimin/al*ly*
submar/ine
sub/mergen*ce*
submis/sive*ly*
sub/mitt*ed*

subordin/at*ed*
sub/orn*ed*
sub/poena*ed*
sub/scrib*ed*
sub/scription
sub/sequent*ly*
subservi/ent
subsid/*ence*
subsidi/ary
subsid/iz*ed*
sub/sidy
subsist/*ence*
sub/stance
substan/tial
substi/tut*ed*
sub/sum*ed*
sub/tend*ed*
subter/fuge
sub/terranean
subtle*ty*
subtly
sub/trac/*tion*
sub/trahend
sub/urb*an*
sub/urb*ia*
subver/sion
sub/vert*ed*
suc/ceed*ed*
success/*ful*
success/*fully*
suc/cessor
suc/cinct*ly*
suc/cour*ed*
succu/lent
suc/cumb*ed*
suc/rose
suc/tion

Sudan/*ese*
sudden/*ness*
su*ed*
suede
suet
suffer/*ance*
suf/fic*ed*
suffi/ciency
suffoca/tion
suffra/gett*e*
suf/fus*ed*
sugar*ed*
suggest/*ible*
sugges/*tion*
sui/cidal
sui/cide
suit/*abil/ity*
suite
suit*or*
sulki/*ness*
sul/lage
sullen/*ness*
sully/*ing*
sulph/ate
sul/phur
sulphur/*ate*
sulphur/*eous*
sul/tan*a*
sul/trily
summar/iz*ed*
sum/mary
sum/mery
summer/sault
     also
     somersault
summit
sum/mon*ed*

sum/mon*ses*

sumptu/ary

sumptu/ous*ly*

sundae*s*

Sun/day

sunder*ed*

sun/dries

sun/nily

super/annu/
  ation

superb*ly*

supercili/ous*ly*

super/eroga/tion

super/fici/ali*ty*

superflu/ity

superflu/ous*ly*

super/intend/*ent*

superi/ori*ty*

superlat/ive*ly*

super/nal

super/natur/al*ly*

super/numerary

super/phosphate

super/saturat*ed*

super/seded*

super/sensitive

supersti/tious*ly*

super/vened*

super/visory

supine

sup/plant*ed*

supplement/*ary*

supple/*ness*

suppli/ant

supplicat/ory

sup/plier

supply/*ing*

support/*able*

sup/pose*d*

supposi/tious

supposit/ory

suppres/s*ion*

suppur/ated*

supra/renal

suprem/acy

su/preme*ly*

sur/cease

sur/charg*ed*

sur/cingl*ed*

sure*ly*

sure*ty*

sur/faced*

surf*ed*

sur/feit*ed*

surg*ed*

sur/geon

sur/gery

surgic/al*ly*

surli/ness

surly

sur/mised*

sur/pass*ed*

sur/plice

sur/plus

sur/pris*ed*

surreal/*ism*

surren/der*ed*

surrepti/tious*ly*

surrey (S)

surrog/ate

sur/rounded*

surtax*ed*

sur/tout

surveil/lance

sur/veyor

sur/vival

sur/vivor

suscept/ible

sus/pect*ed*

sus/pended*

sus/pense

suspens/ible

suspen/sion

suspi/cious*ly*

sus/pired*

sus/tained*

susten/ance

suttee

suture

suzer/ain*ty*

svelte

swab*bed*

swaddl*ed*

swag

swag/ger*ed*

Swa/hili

swain

swal/low*ed*

swami

swamp*ed*

sward

swarm*ed*

swart

swarthi/ness

swarthy

swashbuck/ler

swas/tika

swat*ted* ↔
  swot*ted*

swatch

swath*ed*

swathes *also*
  swath*s*

sweat*ed*

swede

Swedish

sweet/*ener*

swel/ter*ed*

swerv*ed*

swindl*ed*

swinish

swirl*ed*

Swiss

swivel*led*

swizzle

swol/len

swoon*ed*

sword

swore

sworn

swot*ted* ↔
  swat*ted*

sybar/ite

syca/more

sycophan*tic*

syl/labic

syl/lable

sylla/bub *also*
  silla/bub

syl/labuse*s*

syl/logism

sylph

sylvan *also*
  silvan

sylvi/culture
  also silvi/
  culture

sym/bi/osis

symbol/ical
sym/metrical*ly*
sym/metry
sympath/etic
sympath/ize*d*
sym/phony
sym/posium
sympto/m*atic*
syn/agogue
synchro/mesh
synchron/ize*d*
synchron/ous*ly*
synco/pate*d*
syn/cope
syndical/*ism*
syndic/ate
synod
syn/onym/ous*ly*
syn/opsis
syn/optic
synov/itis
syn/tactic
syntax
syn/thesis
synthetic/*ally*
syph/ilis
syr/inge*d*
syrup
sys/taltic
system/*atic*
sys/tole

T

tabard
taber/nacle*d*

tabla/ture
tab/leau*x*
tablet
tab/loid
taboo*ed*
tabor
tabu/lar **a**
tab/ula rasa
tabu/lator
tachisto/scope
tacho/meter
tachy/cardia
tachy/meter
tacit*ly*
taciturn/*ity*
tactic/al*ly*
tacti/*cian*
tact/ile
tactu/al*ly*
tad/pole
taf/feta
tail/*less*
tailor*ed*
taint*ed*
talcum
tal/ent*ed*
talis/man*ic*
talk*at/ive*
tally/*ing*
tally-ho
talon
tamar/ind
tamar/isk
tambour/*ine*
tame/*able*
Tamil

tampan
tampon
tandem
tangen/tial*ly*
tanger/ine
tangible
tangos
tank/ard
tan/*nery*
tan*nic*
tantal/ize*d*
tanta/mount
tan/trum
Taoism
taper*ed*
tapes/try
tapi/oca
tapir
tappet
tap/*ster*
taran/tula*s*
tardi/ness
tare
target
tariff*s*
tarmac
tar/nishe*d*
tar/paulin
tar/ried
tar*ry*
tarsus
tar/tan
tartar (T)
tar/*taric*
tassell*ed*
taste/*able*
taste/*ful*

tasti/est
tasty
tatter*ed*
tattoo*ed*
tatty
taught
taunt*ed*
taur/ine
taut
tauto/log*y*
tavern
tawdry
tawny
tax/*able*
taxie*d*
taxi/dermy
taxi/*ing*
taxi/meter
tax/onomy
teach/*able*
teak
teal
team*ed*
team/*ster*
tease*d*
teasel *also*
   teazel, teazle
teat*ed*
technic/ali*ty*
techni/*cian*
tech/nique
techno/cracy
techno/logical
techno/log*y*
tec/tonic
Te Deum
tedi/ous*ly*

tedium

teed

teemed

teen/ager

teetered

teeth

teethed

tee/total/ler

tee/totum

tele/cast

tele/genic

tele/gram

tele/graphic

tele/kinesis

tele/meter

tele/ology

tele/pathic

tele/phoned

tele/phonist

tele/scoped

tele/vise

tele/vision

tellur/ian

temer/ariously

temer/ity

tem/pera/mental

temper/ately

temperat/ure

tempestu/ous

temp/lar

tem/plate

tempor/ality

tempor/ary

tempor/ized

tempta/tion

ten/able

ten/aciously

tenacu/lum

ten/ancy

tenant/able

tend/ency

tenden/tiously

ten/derer

tendon

ten/dril

tene/brous

tene/ment

tenet

tennis

tenor

tensed

tens/ile

ten/sion

tent/acles

tentat/ively

tenter/hooks

tenu/ously

tenure

te/pee also

    teepee

tepid/ity

ter/centen/ary

termag/ant

termin/able

termin/ally

termin/ator

termino/logy

ter/minus [nuses

   or ni]

termit/ary

ter/mite

tern

ter/raced

terra/cotta

ter/rain

terra/pin

ter/rene

terrest/rial

ter/ribly

ter/rier

terrific/ally

terri/fying

territor/ial

territ/ory

terror/ist

tersely

ter/tiary

Tery/lene

tessel/lated

tes/serae

testament/ary

test/icle

testi/fying

testi/monial

testi/mony

te/tanic

tet/anus

tetchy

tête-/à-tête

tethered

tetra/dactyl

tetra/meter

tex/tile

tex/tual

tex/tured

thal/lium

thane

thatched

thawed

theatre

the/atrical

their ↔ there

theism

them/atic

theme

theo/cratic

theodol/ite

theo/logian

theo/logue

the/orem

theoret/ical

theory

theo/sophy

thera/peutic

ther/apy

there ↔ their

there/fore

ther/mal

thermi/onic

therm/it also

   therm/ite

thermo/

   dynamics

thermo/meter

thermo/static

ther/mos

the/saurus [ri]

thesis [theses]

theta

thicket

thief [thieves]

thiev/ish

thighs

thimble

thin/ness

thirs/tily

thir/teenth

thirti/eth

thistly
thither
thor/acic
thorax
thorough/fare
thor/oughly
thought/ful
thou/sandth
thral/dom
thrall
thrashed also
  threshed
threaded
threatened
thren/ody
threshed also
  thrashed
thresh/old
threw
thrice
thrifty
thrips
thrived
throaty
throb/bing
throes
throm/bosis
throned
throttled
through/out
throve
thrown
thudded
thuggee
thumbed
thunder/ously
Thurs/day

thwarted
thyme
thymus
thyr/oid
thyrox/ine
tiara
tic ↔ tick
tick/eted
tick/lish
tidal
tiddly-/winks
tide
tidi/ness
tied
tierce
tiered
tiff
tiger/ishly
tightened
tike also tyke
tilery
till
tilth
tim/bered
timbre
tim/brel
timid/ity
timor/ously
timpan/ist also
  tym/panist
tinned
tinctured
tined
tinge/ing
tin/gling
tini/est
tink/ling

tinselled
tintinnabu/lation
tiny
Tipper/ary
tipsi/ness
tipsy
tip/toed
tir/ade
tire ↔ tyre
tire/some
'tis
tissues
ti/tanic (T)
ti/tanium
tit/bit
tithed
titil/lated
titiv/ated
titled
ti/trate
tittered
tittle
titu/lar
toad
toady/ing
toasted
tobaccon/ist
tobac/cos
toboggan/ist
toby
tocsin
toddled
toddy
tof/fee
togaed
together/ness
toilet

toil/some
token
toler/able
tolera/tion
tollable
tolled
toma/hawked
toma/toes
tombed
tome
to/morrow
tonally
tonguing
tonic/ally
toni/city
ton/nage
ton/neau
tonsil/litis
tonsor/ial
ton/sure
ton/tine
tooth/ache
topaz
topi
topi/arian
topic/ally
topo/graphical
topo/graphy
topsy-/turvy
toque
tor ↔ torr
Torah
tor/eador
tor/mentor
torna/does
tor/pedoes
torpid/ity

torque
torr ↔ tor
torren/tial*ly*
torrid
tor/sion
torso*s*
tort
tor/tilla
tor/toise
tortu/osity
tortu/ous
tortu/ous*ly*
tor/ture*d*
Tory/*ism*
totali*t/arian*
total/*izator*
to/tal*led*
tote*d*
to/tem*ic*
tot/tery
toucan
toughen*ed*
toupee
tour/*ist*
tourma/line
tourna/ment
tour/neys
tourni/quet
tousle*d*
toute*d*
to/wards
towel/*ling*
tower
tox/aemia
tox/ic*ity*
toxin
toxo/philite

toy*ed*
trace*ry*
tra/chea
trach/oma
tract
tract/able
traction
trac/tor
tradition/al*ly*
traduc/ible
traffic/*able*
traffic/*ator*
traf/ficke*r*
tra/gedian
tra/gedy
tragi/*cally*
tragi/comedy
trait
traitor/*ous*
traject/ory
tram/mel*led*
trampo/line
trance*d*
trans/acto*r*
trans/ceiver
transcend/*ental*
tran/scrip*tion*
tran/sept
trans/fer
transfer/*able*
transfer/*ence*
transferre*d*
transferre*r*
trans/figure*d*
transforma/*tion*

trans/forme*r*
transfu/sion
transgres/*sor*
transi/ent
transistor/ize*d*
transition/al*ly*
transit/ive*ly*
transit/ory
trans/lator
trans/literator
trans/lucent
trans/migratory
transmiss/ible
transmit/*table*
transmit/*tance*
trans/mit*ted*
transmit/*ter*
transmogri/*fying*
trans/mutable
trans/mutation
transpar/ency
tran/spire*d*
transport*able*
trans/posal
transposi/tion
trans-/shipp*ed*
tran/substanti/
  ation
transversal*ly*
trans/verse*ly*
tra/peze
trapez/ium
trapez/oid*al*
trap/*pean*
Trap/pist
trashi/ness
trau/ma*tic*

trav/aile*d*
travelle*d*
travel/*ler*
trav/elogue
tra/versed*d*
trav/esty
trawle*d*
treacher/ous*ly*
treacly
tread*le*
treason/*able*
treas/ure*r*
treas/ury
treat/ise
treaty
treble*d*
tre/foil
trekke*d*
trel/lise*d*
trem/ellose
tremend/ous*ly*
tremor
tremu/lous*ly*
trench/ant*ly*
trencher
trental
tre/pann*ed*
trepida/tion
tres/passe*d*
tresse*s*
trestle
trey
triad
trial
tri/angle
triangu/lar
tribal/*ism*

tri/bal*ly*	trite*ly*	tru/ancy	tu/ition
tribu/lation	tri/theism	*t*ruant	tulip-/tree
tri/bunal	tri/tium	truce	tulle
trib/une	triumph/al*ly*	truckl*ed*	tum/brel *also*
tribu/tary	triumph/ant*ly*	truc/ulent*ly*	tumbril
trice	triumvir/*ate*	trudg*ed*	tumes/cence
trice*ps*	trivet	truism	tumid
trichi/na*e*	trivi/al*ity*	truly	tumour
trich/osis	triv/ium	trump/ery	tumultu/ous*ly*
tricho/tomy	tro/chaic	trum/pet*ed*	tumu/lus
trickl*ed*	tro/chee	trun/cat*ed*	tun
triclin/ium	troch/oid*al*	trun/cheon	tuna
tri/colour	trodd*en*	trundl*ed*	tundra*s*
tricot	troglo/dyte	truss*ed*	tune/ful*ly*
tri/cycl*ed*	troika	trust*ee*	tung-/tree
tri/dent	Trojan	trusty	tun/nell*ed*
tried	troll*ed*	truths	tunny
tri/enni/al*ly*	trol/ley*s*	try*ing*	turban*ed*
trier	trol/lop	tryp/sin	turbid/*ity*
trifl*ed*	trom/bone	tryst*ed*	tur/bine
trig/ger*ed*	trope	tsar *also*	turbot
trigono/metry	trophy	czar	turbu/lent*ly*
trilby	trop/ical	tsetse	tur/een
trilob/ite	tropo/sphere	tuba	turf*ed*
tri/logy	trott*ed*	tubb*ed*	turgid*ly*
tri/meter	troth	tuber	Turkey
trim/ming*s*	trouba/dour	tubercle	Turk/*ish*
trin/ity	trouble/*some*	tubercu/lar	turmeric
trin/ket	troub/lous	tubercu/losis	tur/moil
trio*s*	trough	tubercu/lous	turnip
tripart/ite	trouncing	tuber/ose	turn/stile
trip/le*t*	trouper	tubu/lar	turpi/tude
triplic/at*ed*	trousers	tucker	tur/quoise
tripod	trous/seau*s*	tucket	tur/ret*ed*
trip/tych	trove	Tu/dor	turtle
tri/sect*ed*	trowell*ed*	Tues/day	Tus/cany
tri/syllable	troy	tuft*ed*	tusk*y*

tussled
tus/sock
tussore
tutel/age
tutel/ary
tutor/ial
tutti-/frutti
tutu
tu-/whit tu-/
  whoo
twaddled
tweaked
tweedy
tweeted
tweezer
twelfth
twelve
twenti/eth
twiddled
twice
twi/light
twinged
twink/ling
twinned
twirled
twitched
twit/tered
'twixt
two/some
'twould
tycoon
tying
tyke *also* tike
tym/panist *also*
  timpan/ist
tym/panum [na]
typed

type/writer
typh/oid*al*
ty/phoon
typhus
typ/ical
typi/fy*ing*
typist
typo/graphy
tyran/nical
tyran/niz*ed*
tyran/nous*ly*
tyr/anny
tyrant
tyre ↔ tire
Tyro/lese

U

ubi/quitous
ubi/quity
udder*ed*
uku/leles
ulcer/*ous*
ulster (U)
ulter/ior
ulti/mate*ly*
ulti/matum [ta
  or tums]
ultra/marine
ultra/montane
ultra/mundane
ultra/sonic
ultra/violet
ulu/lat*ed*
umber
umbil/icus

umbrage
um/brella
umpire
unanim/ity
unanim/ous*ly*
un/couth*ly*
unc/tion
unctu/ous*ly*
under/neath
under/rate
undies
un/doubted
undu/latory
un/duly
ungual
un/guent
ungu/la*te*
uni/corn
uniform/*ity*
unify/*ing*
uni/lateral
union/*ism*
union/*ist*
unique/*ness*
unison
unit/*arian*
unity
universal/*ity*
uni/verse
univer/sity
un/kempt
un/neces/sary
un/remit/ting
un/requited
un/rivalled
until
un/usual

un/wieldy
Upan/ishad
up/braid*ed*
up/heaval
uphol/ster*ed*
upper/most
up*pish*
upright/*ness*
uproari/ous*ly*
ur/anium
Uranus
urban
urbane
urban/ity
urban/iz*ed*
urchin
Urdu
urea
ureter
ureth/ral
urgent*ly*
uric
urinal
urn*ed*
ursine
urtic/aria
usage
usance
usher/*ette*
usu/all*y*
usurious/*ness*
usurp*ed*
usury
uten/sil
uter/ine
uterus
utilit/arian/*ism*

util/ity
util/ized
utmost
uto/pian (U)
utter/ance
uvula
uxori/ously

V

va/cancy
vacated
vaca/tion
vaccin/ated
vac/cine
vacil/lated
vacu/ity
vacu/ole
vacu/ously
vacuum
vagabond/age
vagary
vaginal
vag/rancy
vaguely
vain ↔ vane,
  vein
val/ance also
  val/ence
vale ↔ veil
vale/dictory
val/ence also
  val/ance
valency
valen/tine
va/lerian

valet
valetudin/arian
Val/halla
vali/antly
valid/ity
valise
Valkyrie
valleys
valor/ously
valour
valu/able
valued
valve
valv/ular
vam/pire
vana/dium
vandal/ism
van/dyke
vane ↔ vain,
  vein
van/guard
va/nilla
van/ity
vanquish/able
vant/age
vapid/ity
vapor/ized
vapor/ous
vapour
va/queros
vari/able
vari/ance
vari/ation
vari/coloured
varic/ose
varie/gated
vari/eties

vari/ety
vari/olar
vario/meter
vari/orum
vari/ously
varlet
var/nished
vary/ing
vascu/lar
vase
vasel/ine (V)
vassal/age
vastly
Vat/ican
vaude/ville
vaulted
vaunted
veal
vector
veered
vegan
Vege/mite
veget/able
veget/arian
vegeta/tion
vehe/mently
vehicle
vehicu/lar
veil ↔ vale
vein ↔ vain,
  vane
veld also
  veldt
vellum
velo/city
velours
velvet/een

venal
vena/tion
ven/detta
vendor
veneered
vener/able
venera/tion
vener/eal
ven/geance
vene/tian
  (V)
venial/ity
Venice
ven/ison
venom/ously
venous
ventil/ator
vent/ral
vent/ricle
ventri/loquial
ventri/loquism
venture/some
venue
Venus
vera/cious
vera/city
ver/anda also
  ver/andah
verb/ally
verba/tim
ver/bena
verbi/age
verb/osely
verbos/ity
verd/ancy
ver/dict
verdi/gris

ver/dure
verged
verger
veri/fying
verily
veri/similit/ude
verit/able
verity
vermi/celli
vermilion
vermin/ous
ver/mouth
vernacu/lar
vernal
ver/onal
veron/ica
vers libre
versat/ilely
verse
versifica/tion
ver/sion
versus
verteb/rae
verteb/rate
vertex [tices]
vertic/ally
vertigin/ous
verti/gos
verve
ves/icle
vespers
vespi/ary
vessel
vestal
vesti/bule
vest/iges
vesti/gial

vestry
ves/ture
Vesuv/ian
vet/eran
veterin/ary
vetoes
vexa/tiously
via
viable
via/duct
vial
viands
viat/icum
vi/brant
vi/brating
vibrat/ory
vi/burnum
vicar/age
vicari/ously
vice
vice versa
vice/regal
vice/roy
vicin/ity
vi/ciously
vicissi/tude
victim/ized
victori/ously
victualled
vicuña
vied
Vien/nese
viewed
vigil/ance
vigil/antes
vignette
vigor/ous

vigour
Viking
vilely
vili/fying
villa
villain/ous
villein/age
vinai/grette
vin/cible
vincu/lum
vindic/atory
vindict/ively
vineg/ary
vine/yard
vin/tage
vint/ner
viola
viol/able
viol/ator
viol/ence
violet
violin/ist
violon/cellos
viper/ishly
vira/gos
vir/gate
virgin/ity
viri/descent
virilely
viril/ity
viro/logy
virtu
virtu/ally
virtue
virtu/oso
virtu/ously

viru/lently
viruses
visa
vis/age
vis-à-vis
vis/ceral
viscid/ity
vis/cose
vis/count
visibil/ity
vis/ible
vision/ary
vis/itor
visor
vistas
visual/ized
visu/ally
vital/ity
vit/amin
viti/ated
vitre/ous
vitri/olic
vituperat/
ively
viva/ciously
viva/city
vivar/ium
viva-/voce
vivid/ness
vivi/fying
vivi/parous
vivi/section
vixen/ish
vizier
vocabu/lary
vocal/ized
vocation/ally

vocifer/ously
vodka
vogue
voice/less
voided
voile
volat/ile
volca/noes
vole
voli/tional
volleys
volt/age
vol/taic
volta/meter
volte-/face
voluble
volume
volu/metric
volumin/ously
voluntar/ily
volun/tary
volun/teered
voluptu/ary
vom/ited
vomit/ory
voodooed
vora/ciously
vor/texes
  [tices]
votary
voucher
vouch/safed
vowel/ized
voy/ager
vulcan/ite
vulgar/ity
vul/gate (V)

vulner/able
vulp/ine
vul/ture
vying

W

wad/ding
waddled
waddy
wadi
wafer
waffled
wafted
wag/gish
wagon/ette also
  waggon/ette
waifs
wainscot/ing
waisted
wait/ress
waived
walk/about
walkie-/talkie
wallaby [bies]
walla/roo
wallet
walloped
wallowed
walnut
walruses
waltzed
wam/pum
wan/derer
wander/lust
waned

wan/ness
wanton
wanton/ness
warb/ler
warden
ward/robe
ware
war/fare
war/ily
war/lock
warmth
warn/ing
warped
war/ranty
warren
war/rior
warty
wary
wash/able
wasp/ish
was/sailer
wastage
waste/fully
wastrel
watered
watery
watt/age
wattle
wavi/ness
wavy
waxy
way/farer
way/ward
weakened
weak/ling
weakly
weal

weald
wealthy
weaned
weapon
wear/able
weari/ness
weari/some
weary
weasel
weathered
weatherly
weaver
web/bing
wed/ding
wedged
Wedgwood
wed/lock
Wednes/day
weekly
wee/vily
weft
weigh
weighty
weir
weirdly
welched also
  welshed
welcom/ing
wel/fare
wel/kin
welling/tons
Welsh
welshed also
  welched
welted
weltered
wen

wench

were/wolf
[wolves]

west/*erly*

west/*ern*

West/minster

wether

wet*ted*

whack

whack*ed*

whack*er*

whal*er*

wharf [wharves]

wharf/*age*

what/soever

wheat*en*

wheedl*ed*

wheel*ed*

wheez/*ily*

whelk*ed*

whelp*ed*

whence/soever

when/ever

where/abouts

wher/ever

where/withal

wherry

whether

whet*ted*

whey

Whig/*gery*

whilst

whim

whim/per*ed*

whimsey *also*
whimsy

whimsic/al*ly*

whinge*ing* *also*
whing*ing*

whing*er*

whining*ly*

whinny/*ing*

whip/pet

whirl*ed*

whirr

whirr*ed*

whisky

whis/per*ed*

whistl*ed*

whit

whiten/*ing*

whither

whit/ing

whit/low

whittl*ed*

whiz *also* whizz

whizz*ed*

whole/sal*er*

whole/some*ly*

wholly

who*m*

whoop/*ing*-/
cough

whop/*ping*

whor*ed*

whorl*ed*

who's

whose

wicker

wicket

widen*ed*

widgeon *also*
wigeon

wid/ow*er*

width

wield*ed*

wigeon *also*
widgeon

wigwam

wilde/beest

wild*er*/*ness*

wil*es*

wil/ful*ly*

wili/ness

willowy

willy-/nilly

wily

Wimbledon

wimpl*ed*

winc*ed*

wind/*ily*

wind/lass*es*

win/nings

winnow*ed*

win/some*ly*

winter*ed*

wintry

wire/*less*

wiri/ness

wiry

wise/acre

wispi/ness

wispy

wis/taria *also*
wis/teria

wist/ful*ly*

witch/*ery*

witch/etty

witena/gemot

withal

with/draw*al*

withe *also* withy

wither*ed*

wither/shins

with/hold

withy *also* withe

wit/ness*ed*

wit*ti*/cism

wit/*tily*

wit/*tingly*

wit*ty*

wiz/ardry

wiz/en*ed*

woad

wobbl*ed*

woe/begone

woe/ful*ly*

wold

wolf [wolves]

wolfish/*ness*

wolf/ram

wolver/ine

woman [women]

womb

wombat

wonder/*ful*

wonder/ful*ly*

won/drous*ly*

won't

wont*ed*

wood/chuck

wooden/*ness*

woody

woo*ed*

woof

wool/*len*

wool*ly*

worldly

worm-/eaten
worry/*ing*
worsen*ed*
wor/ship*ped*
worst*ed*
wor/thily
worthy
woven
wrack
wrangl*ed*
wrap/*per*
wrath/ful*ly*
wreak
wreath **n**
wreath*ed* **v**
wreck/*age*
wrench*ed*
wrest*ed*
wrestl*ed*
wretch*ed*
wrick *also* rick
wrier *also*
  wry*er*
wriggl*ed*
wright
wring*er*
wrinkl*ed*
wrist/*let*
writ
write
writh*ed*
writing
writ/ten
wrong/do*er*
wrong*ed*
wrote
wroth

wrought-/iron
wrung
wry*er* *also*
  wrier
wry/*ness*

X

xebec
xenon
xeno/phobia
xero/graphy
x-ray*ed* (X)
xylon/ite
xylo/phone

Y

yacht*ing*
yahoo
Yahveh *also*
  Yahweh
yak
yam
Yankee
yar/borough
yash/mak
yaw*ed*
yawl
yawn*ed*
yaws
yea
yeah
year*ly*
yearn*ed*

yeast*y*
yellow/*ing*
yen **s/p**
yeo/man*ry*
yeti
yew
Yid/dish
yield*ed*
ylang-/ylang
yo/del*led*
yoga
yog/hurt *also*
  yog/urt
yogi
yoicks
yoke
yokel
yolk
yore
york*er*
York/shire
young/*ster*
youth/ful*ly*
ytter/bium
yt/trium
yucca
Yugo/slav*ia*
yule/tide

Z

zaffre
zany
Zanzi/bar
zealo*t*
zeal/*ous*

zebra*s*
zebu*s*
Zeit/geist
zemin/dar
ze/nana
zenith
ze/olite
zephyr*s*
Zep/pelin
zero*s*
zest/ful*ly*
Zeus
zig/zag*ged*
zinc*ed* *also*
  zinc*ked*
zinc*y* *also* zinky
zinnia*s*
Zion/*ist*
zip*ped*
zirco/n*ium*
zither
zodi/ac*al*
zombie*s*
zonal
zoolo/gical
zo/ology
zoom*ed*
Zouave
zuc/chetto
zuc/chini
Zulu*s*
zwie/back
zygote
zy/mosis

OTHER TITLES IN THE SERIES